Common Life

Common Life

by Stéphane Bouquet
translated by Lindsay Turner

Nightboat Books
New York

This work received the French Voices Award for excellence
in publication and translation. French Voices is a program
created and funded by the French Embassy in the United
States and FACE Foundation.

ISBN: 978-1-643-62153-1

Cover art: *Ritual Group Drawing Score*, Experiments in
Environment workshop, Sea Ranch, CA, July 6th, 1968
Lawrence Halprin Collection, The Architectural Archives,
University of Pennsylvania

Design and typesetting by Rissa Hochberger
Typeset in Caslon 540

Cataloging-in-publication data is available
from the Library of Congress

Nightboat Books
New York
www.nightboat.org

Contents

I.   *Fraternally*

AS AN EXCUSE

I'm thinking of a little poem about the one who wondered
        what pills I was taking
at night. Pills against absence. He's sitting
        so close oh I'd love
to write one more sadness on the inaccessible shelter
        of his shoulders. Of course
a friend has generously emailed to let me know
        he thinks my poems are mostly
narcissistic tactics of seduction. Isn't it worth writing, then,
        the stormy morning
in Vienna, the acacias aimed directly over us, or
        the club
with the Bulgarian prostitutes, the night before, when
        we danced
pressed up against humanity's minor bodies? Not worth writing
and nothing to do with the future of living? Possibly—but then
        listen my interior troubadours
I hear them crying *oyez oyez* pleasure each time
        I sing
my least particular lady. Him, for example. He makes the world
vibrate faster, he gives us a
        deeper winter: look
the trees in the courtyard, naked and straight in their bark and
        duration. It's like
entering a season awakened by need: it isn't certain
        that the sidewalks
help you balance but if you manage right
        his face
can help you walk the streets. Who is it who once said, "existence
        is nothing but the declension
of bodies?" No one, maybe. And yet it's true: everything
        tries
to pull a piece off of the embrace. Let's say a dove
        pulls a worm out of the earth
and you raise someone's arm and smell his armpit then
        the rest comes too,

when through deductions or inductions even tomorrow
        turns green again and we become
approximable. He, for example, who's now just
        a faraway face,
I'm learning to breathe in absence and with deferred lungs.
        And then this morning
a researcher on the radio explained that we already know how
        to make 3D biophotocopies
of bits of skin and cornea—so let me
just copy your body and I promise then to leave the original
        alone. In any case
my friends I'm writing less and less poetry. I'm only adding
        words to days
hoping to get past the intense odor
        of solitude
stagnating ceaselessly beneath my arms—and then more salvos
from the interior troubadours: keep on, keep on weaving verses
        to the only truth
there is, to the stupor of existing. And so the gulls climb again
        over the land, following
the rivers from landfill to landfill, because
        they're good examples
of adjectives: avid, famished, starving, and the whole
        linguistic list
that means simply, I miss you. What you?
        I told you yesterday, the smallest
member of the universal face. Indeed with you or all of you
        we could be caught up in
the world's talons, if that metaphor makes any sense. It's what
happens to Ganymede, in the myth, an eagle grabs him and he
        drops him off
in the counter-universe of things or the universe of counter-things,
        anyway, I hope we
understand each other: it's just that he learns to close
        the circumference around himself
like certain people roll up in their bedspreads
        or in the adolescent smell

4

of hope and it seems for a second like nothing can escape
        from now on: not
yesterday's living postcard—full moon on the roaring sea
        & the squall whipping
at the windows—not this train not anything. In five, six days
        I'll recognize him: one
of the millions able to stitch or join
        the skin like sometimes
the moss climbs all the way to the corrugated metal roofs and
        we wonder
where it finds the energy to explode so wildly
        in a hostile environment. For example
it's death or death is growing but I'm
        carting around this photocopy
of you or all of you and it's the mask or maybe the wetsuit
        I needed
not to end up already, let's say, suffocated by polluted dust.

ELEGY AGAIN

I declare solitude
        open—the real inauguration of
the littlest world.
It could be anywhere, maybe sitting in this park where
        for the first time
ever in your life you hear the chainsaw sound of a squirrel
        attacking
a nutshell. Here's our little draft of dialogue:
        —Hey, listen, here's what the weather is tomorrow.
There could be a surprise with it
        —Such as?
such as the two kids selling the mushrooms
        they picked themselves
in the woods, resting their crate on a giant plastic tractor.
        They're as
striking as childhood itself, which always asks for something more:
        buy me,
call me, bring me a hand. Well that was the time when hands
had promised to. And now in Brussels, Place de la Bourse,
        gray at 9 am
and on strike so there's much less traffic, someone
        already boozy rooster red
apologizes, "Everybody has to eat," well, ok go ahead and
        in the next streets
persist promises of utopian socialism, promises I know
        how to make last
on demand. And yet what's this strange joy
        even quasi-beatific
of living: things are breathing peacefully, hedges
        trimmed in a certain
logical rigor, as per the will of
        Le Nôtre or someone like that, hedges lately
redone in calm gravel alleys where lovers on their walks
        are separated
by the agonies of brand-name kisses and of
        luxury caresses

and expensive blowjobs, and they know better than I do
        how to cross this street without running
since the streetlight's rarely ever red. And so the solitary tomorrows
        accumulate.
One day in Lorient, along the sheltered basins where the boats
        float dead and covered
in green lichen through which their silhouettes are still recognizable
        —Sailboat!
any child armed with words could still say, words that pretty much
        arrange the world in classificatory
sentences, not
        —Face!
steps to climb on since they might collapse and slide
        into the unsanitary waters
of the port. For honestly these could be just
        some crazy lines
of love intended for the manager of disorder, designed
        to lure him
into his own trap.
You think it's a disaster but it's only
        an illusion.
If you can find it there's a sort of syllabic secret in all this.
        —What?
But I prefer to not know for a second, for the incessant duration
        of a moment, if ever
and if only he'd return and put it all in sweetest order. Is it
        really better to live
in the sentence "I love you" than in "It's morning and it's marvelous
        due to
the vibrant thickness once again entrusted to us by the light?"
        I'm terribly afraid
it is. Now it's time for coffee. Now
        the grounds at the bottom of the cup,
the pot, to throw out with the rest, with those sentences
        that take the place of the very simple ones
where we could live. In any case,
        I'm going to make

this ridiculous chaotic noise for just as long as your disappearance
         remains temporary. Well I know it's
already permanent but these days I only live in
         your direction.
Imagine the earthquake a river would require to be turned out
         of bed, especially if the bed
is yours. Did I tell you about the teenager
who was looking for a light
         but I don't smoke.
Sorry. He seemed to have understood what kinds of signs
         to emit
in order to arrange the looks of others. Did I tell you the secret
         of the syllables? Tonight
I just noticed, and I'm not even exaggerating, that the sky's peach
         and strawberry have mixed
and flow down onto the spires of Notre Dame, our Lady. Our
         is a pronoun
that works for everything. For example
our breath of our hello of our first
         of our morning oh
finally it's all useless in the undulations of the sky,
         the splendor accumulated
for nothing, did I tell you about the fog, white and dense
         on the Styrian Alps,
the slightest sound was soaked in it, and silence, all sound
         perishable and then dead
as soon as it leaves the lips. Considering that your absence
         started at the beginning
and lasted until the day nor the hour—considering
         that words are terribly frail,
incapable of making the crossing—and they drown,
         and silence.

WITHOUT

We must always alight on the livingness of things. At
　　　　breakfast, someone:
"the winters are warming so the electrical companies
　　　　make less
profit." Or else they're going to destroy an
　　　　unprofitable hospital
and its precious art brut frescoes. "Oh no!" says
　　　　common indignation, but yes,
though if I watch mostly the splendor of moats beneath
　　　　the oblique and hesitating
light of morning, perhaps the sky has Sunday
　　　　as its only actual project, before there were
dozens of ducks, where are they, the tearful
　　　　owner's sigh, what's left
is the noisy profusion of insects trees and their foliage
　　　　feeble respite even
if I wanted to say it's fully snowing today, I
　　　　mean that
quasi-pharmaceutical protective powder
　　　　naturally preventing
fear. It is not however going to snow at all but there are
　　　　lots of soldiers
in the streets these days, a sort of consolation prize
　　　　like living
in an unhurtable bulletproof vest. In the end poet =
　　　　the indefatigable maker
of shield-sentences behind which to hide to
　　　　re-calm gently,
the calm of safe and sound. What is it to live? This time
　　　　etymology
isn't going to be much help. In Indo-European to live
　　　　already meant, it seems, to live
and nothing else. Back to the beginning. Perhaps it's
　　　　enough to accumulate a bunch of gestures
and see what the meaning is at the end. Or not meaning:
　　　　"apricot trees exist,

apricot trees exist" (Inger Christensen) and there isn't any
        useful meaning. One day
the jellyfish in turn found that their form
        fit the circumstances
and stayed in it. That's what matters: to sink into the ideal
        or provisionally ideal
form. Of course these days
        the Marie Antoinettes
of the financial aristocracy
        stuff themselves with gluten-free
brioche: "oh little spelt," she purrs, swooning on her silken divan,
        body chiseled
to a monied svelte. In the end it is perhaps better
        that the world just melts
as fast as possible. There'll be a new flood—I apologize
        to all the sacrificed
species, polar bear and monk seal, I
        am sorry—then a neo-Greek
will come to explain the two fundamental reasons
        for being, *ousia* as
the ancient Aristotle said, matter without actual project but
        full of desire
the foremost being, I need badly to caress you.
Everything happens in Syntagma Square,
the great hopefulness of assembled
        sentences.
—Come, he says, we must learn to add up in this
        bereft world,
imagine the inauguration of the without republic: without the
        lazy possibility
of landscapes, I mean where to laze and lounge,
        the banks
abruptly shut by unilateral decree as if the
        reserves of saliva were
exhausted or uncertain, without a certain number
        of promises

nevertheless marvelously to be kept, without the light
of evening when the sun
                wastes us
generously, at our backs, without a single name to call,
                without general strike
or the consolation of back alleys where the stray cats
                wander
without the list of all the rest which I cut short and which was truly
                also possible.

II.   *Monsters*

Play for eleven actors
or more, or fewer

Characters

- CLÉMENT
- MÉLISSA
- VLADILEN
- AMINE
- MANON (THE GOVERNMENT EMPLOYEE)
- COCO
- AURÉLIE
- KEVIN (THE BARE-CHESTED GUY)
- FRANCK PROJOT
- VÉRA
- HÉLENE

NEIGHBORS, COLLEAGUES, FRIENDS

- AN INTELLECTUAL COUPLE (A WOMAN, A MAN)
- MYRTILLE
- THE CLOTHED GUY
- THE WRITER
- THE WOMAN IN THE PINK JACKET
- THE WOMAN IN THE BLUE CARDIGAN
- THE HOUSEKEEPER
- MARK (ONLINE VOICE 1)
- TANGUY (ONLINE VOICE 2)

THE DISTANT

- THE SAFARI COUPLE (A WOMAN, A MAN)
- THE OTHER HOUSEKEEPER
- THE VOICES OF WORK
- THE ORDINARY CITIZEN

1.

A couple in their kitchen. It doesn't matter whether the man or the woman speaks first.

We should make sure they've inspected the car.

I guess they probably only rent cars they already inspected.

I don't know. It's still . . . I read that these people . . . their car broke down in the middle of the bush, they found them a few days later half-devoured by the animals.

Half only? The rest wasn't any good?

Well anyway, even if they cleaned off all the bones the animals wouldn't have swallowed everything. After a while someone would've remembered, maybe. Or some twenty-fourth century historian studying early twenty-first century tourist culture would find the article and become obsessed with them. I remember there were some pictures in the paper.

I don't think fate has anything so marvelously exceptional in store for us. We'll get on the plane. There will be no terrorists, no depressive pilot, no defective motor, no thunderstorm to bring us down. The car is going to work fine. We'll see lions, antelopes, zebras, giraffes, elephants, maybe monkeys. Whenever there's service we'll post selfies with animals in the background. Look, there were monkeys in these lush green trees but we were never quick enough to catch them in motion.

If we know everything in advance, maybe it's not worth going.

You're just scared to travel. For the whole time I've known you—the night before the trip it's back pain, stomachaches, bronchitis . . .

That time you had to carry both our backpacks because I

couldn't, and we basically crawled from one end of the station to the other.

That time, and others.

Do you remember when we were in the Topkapi Palace, and we saw that old poem carved into the stone?

What does that have to do with anything?

I saw the reflection of your face in the window, and your acne scars, and I said to myself how right I was to be traveling with you and that I would never regret a thing.

(Embracing each other) Tomorrow morning we have to remember to set up our email away messages.

Gone but back on the fifteenth.

We'll definitely be back.

2.

A woman writes a letter.

AURÉLIE:

Dear you ten,

I'm sitting on a little wooden dock. My legs are dangling in the water, which is awfully warm because of global warming. The river is called the Danube. After work people come here in swarms like wasps, humming sweetly . . . buzz buzz buzz . . . I don't understand German, but it doesn't really matter. They're tan and delicious around their slices of mortadella, jumping diving splashing laughing eating caressing loving. It seems like some of them could go on forever. When I was swimming just now, with my goggles on, there were these immense marbled carp gliding beneath me, my ride into prehistory. I'm alone in language but it's okay, believe me. I can't get over it: swimming in the word Danube, in Vienna, in this word that lives up to its legend. My dear ten, the water's so nice. It's as warm as the chandeliers, the balls, the waltzes, the saddest feeling of being Sissi. Station: Alte Donau. On the horizon, the light scattered by the glass windows of the buildings in the financial district.

Love,
Aurélie, the eleventh.

3.

The intellectual couple, driving or pretending to be driving.

SHE: Fresh-picked berries! Should we get some?

HE: The boys are sleeping and the car is full. Where do you want to put them?

SHE: Down by my feet.

HE: You'll step on them and get annoyed.

SHE: *(Turning back to look at the boys)* Well anyway, they're beautiful. Sometimes I think that if we hadn't had kids we could have done other things. We could have taken a safari, like the neighbors—you know they left yesterday. They left me a message before they went, and last they checked the cats are okay and the fish are okay and they hadn't seen the turtle in a little while, but she must be gorging herself on the long grass in the backyard. Can a turtle get so fat that she won't be able to go back in her shell?

HE: If the boys were ugly, would you have regretted not going on safari?

SHE: *(Takes a minute to think both sides of it)* Honestly, I think so, yes. You don't have kids if you're going to pro-duce monsters.

HE: Their eyes are closed but it doesn't mean they're sleeping.

SHE: I just said they were beautiful! Life's been good to us, knock on wood. There's no wood in this car but knock on wood in my head. I'm knocking on the big oak beside the house. What's going to happen?

HE: "We shall live, you and I. We shall live out many, many days and long evenings; we shall patiently bear out the trials fate sends us," Chekhov.

SHE: I don't think I could ever stand living with anyone other than you. You always have the right quotation for the right moment. I'm not being sarcastic. You're like a sort of medicine cabinet.

HE: On the other hand, we've been little too sheltered in our books. We let the days go by without touching them. We haven't really gotten our hands dirty. Literally, I mean, we can go days without showering because we move so little.

SHE: We like our own smell. We like to wallow in our own smell, that's all.

HE: We're like that dog family.

SHE: Dog 1 and dog 2, in the same boat.

HE: That makes me think of this Danish artist who made a pharmacy out of words. Healing words, holy words, a doctor's kit of words that cure. I could get you that for our anniversary.

SHE: That first summer, in the house, when Ralph and Eugénie brought you with them as a surprise and when we decided to study for the exam together, I stole your dirty laundry and I took it to my room and I breathed it.

HE: Why did we have kids?

SHE: They might not be sleeping.

HE: We had kids because life was so peaceful it was getting dangerous.

SHE: You really remember that or you'd like to remember that?

HE: You mean that, in fact, we were afraid of failing the exams and we didn't know how to survive. Our parents were bugging us. Mark was an accident. Probably. But that's the only reason to get older. You can drown everything in the lukewarm water of memory.

SHE: Everything. Almost everything, yes.

4.

An apartment.

THE BARE-CHESTED GUY: Want to suck my dick?

THE CLOTHED GUY: *(Already making coffee)* No . . . no . . . should I make us some coffee?

THE BARE-CHESTED GUY: Sure, but it'll be the same price.

THE CLOTHED GUY: No worries.

THE BARE-CHESTED GUY: Can I sit down?

THE CLOTHED GUY: Yes. You're beautiful to look at.

THE BARE-CHESTED GUY: So you're a sociologist and you're doing research on sex workers. You're a social worker and you want to get to know the people you work with better. You're the sworn-in representative of monotheism and God, who speaks through your mouth and has come to reveal to me that I've chosen the wrong path. I have no desire to respond to you.

THE CLOTHED GUY: No . . . I just wanted us to have coffee.

THE BARE-CHESTED GUY: Then you could have asked anyone off the street.

THE CLOTHED GUY: Strangers are scared of me. They think I'd drug the coffee in order to rob them or rape them.

THE BARE-CHESTED GUY: Whereas with me, for the price you're paying, you could actually drug the coffee and rape me.

THE CLOTHED GUY: I just wanted to make you coffee. And I don't like to go out in the streets.

THE BARE-CHESTED GUY: You don't even want me to get naked?

THE CLOTHED GUY: No. Nothing against you. Your beauty is considerable.

THE BARE-CHESTED GUY: I'm not really very comfortable, dressed in front of a client.

THE CLOTHED GUY: If you want you can go to sleep. I'll wake you up in an hour. If you can manage to sleep—if you can feel unusually serene and light and safe—that would make me happy.

THE BARE-CHESTED GUY: In the movies there'd be a close-up of my face, which couldn't be more surprised.

THE CLOTHED GUY: I don't go to the movies anymore.

THE BARE-CHESTED GUY: That's a mistake.

THE CLOTHED GUY: I tell myself: if someone is paid by the hour and forgets that hour, forgets time . . . if that person prefers peace here over money elsewhere . . . is there anything more . . . doesn't that make the world more peaceful?

THE BARE-CHESTED GUY: They drink their coffee.

5.

A salon, white tiles, air full of creams and lotions. A woman speaking into her telephone.

MÉLISSA:

Dear you ten,

Barely just back from vacation and it's 1 pm–9 pm, Saturdays too. Mélissa this and Mélissa that. I get upset and slam the door and then send my best I'm-sorry smile towards the client in the massage chair with her feet in the basin. "Not too hot?" The client shakes her head no and closes her eyes in pleasure. Feet in a sorry state thanks to the heels management requires: company code, hostess section. Brothers & Brothers hello. No one ever rubs your feet? I ask her gently because I can tell when women want to talk and cry. I give the women who come here feet of silk. Feet of silk on the outside and feet of steel on the inside. Not because of We the Women but because I know what it's like, when I get home and turn on the lights, when the cat comes and rubs against my legs, finally, you get it. Now she's crying. She's crying over something that happened to her, divorce or cancer or being laid off. It doesn't matter what if I want to console her. Look, it's September. No one's really worried about the leaves falling. Same with us. We all fall equally in a forest of indifference. But maybe I'm wrong. For example, a class of schoolchildren walks in the woods and gathers and arranges, one beside the other: an oak leaf, a maple leaf, an elm leaf, a chestnut leaf, a beech leaf, a birch leaf, a plane tree leaf, an ash leaf, a hazel leaf, a poplar leaf. One of each type of leaf growing in the common forest.

To us,
Mélissa, the eleventh.

6.

Hotel rooms. The two women are working in 501 and 502.

THE OTHER HOUSEKEEPER: What'd you do yesterday?

THE HOUSEKEEPER: We watched Channel 2.

THE OTHER HOUSEKEEPER: Oh I've got Channel 1. I saw the show for 2 but thought it was the same. Was it good?

THE HOUSEKEEPER: I fell asleep, I got . . .

THE OTHER HOUSEKEEPER: . . . woken up by the commercials?

THE HOUSEKEEPER: No, Kevin was snoring.

THE OTHER HOUSEKEEPER: But he's not fat! *(The other says, "no," but the first is already continuing)* The fatter you are the more you snore. I read it in the paper on the train. When you gain weight even the base of your tongue gets fat and it blocks your throat, the . . . I forget what it's called. Anyway, snoring.

THE HOUSEKEEPER: Anyway, he isn't fat.

THE OTHER HOUSEKEEPER: No, Kevin's cute.

THE HOUSEKEEPER: *(Politely)* Well Riccardo's not bad either. *(No response)* Riccardo's not bad either.

THE OTHER HOUSEKEEPER: Look what I just found.

She holds a wallet in her hand.

THE HOUSEKEEPER: Call the supervisor?

THE OTHER HOUSEKEEPER: Or we can keep it.

THE HOUSEKEEPER: The guest calls and you say what, that you didn't find it? I have to warn you, I'm not good at lying.

THE OTHER HOUSEKEEPER: Or that he must have left it somewhere else, but it wasn't in the room.

THE HOUSEKEEPER: I heard that management sometimes sets traps. They put valuables out and if you don't return them you're fired.

The other doesn't answer.

THE HOUSEKEEPER: Did you hear me? Then you're fired and you're unemployed again and your ex asks for custody and gets it and then they're going to say that I get thieves hired.

THE OTHER HOUSEKEEPER: They plant a diamond and you steal a diamond. You take off your good little busy cleaning bee outfit and go out the back door. You sell the diamond back in Anvers, that's where they sell diamonds, you flee to a foreign country. Anyway you just earned more than in your entire stupid life dusting rooms.

THE HOUSEKEEPER: Yeah but the international police follow your ass. You get caught, no one knows how to hide from the international police. You get extradited. You're back.

THE OTHER HOUSEKEEPER: You say you don't know how to lie. You don't know how to lie, ok, but before you met Kevin you lied to enough guys.

THE HOUSEKEEPER: A guy who doesn't deserve to be lied to, that's how you know you love him. Wait. Maybe I've got an idea. Maybe you take it back without any money in it. We can say you found it in the hallway.

THE OTHER HOUSEKEEPER: *(Silence, thinking)* Yes . . .
but . . . fingerprints, that's a problem. My prints will be there
and the client's but if there's no one else's—from the thief—
I'm done for.

THE HOUSEKEEPER. Ah. You're right.

THE OTHER HOUSEKEEPER: See. TV is good for something.

THE HOUSEKEEPER: Plus there are cameras in the hallways.
Okay, call him.

THE OTHER HOUSEKEEPER: Anyway we're stuck. Any-
where you see a little bit of cheese sticking out somewhere
you can be sure there's a metal door about to come down right
on your nose. Everywhere. Everywhere in the world. They're
scared of the Revolution.

THE HOUSEKEEPER: That's just what Riccardo says.

THE OTHER HOUSEKEEPER: That's what Riccardo says but
that's what I say too. Look at the refugees. They say they don't
want them here and that we're overwhelmed, but actually they're
glad, because that means they can keep lowering the wages.

A bell rings.

THE HOUSEKEEPER: Oh god, I'm running half a room late.
Call that piece of shit.

7.

A man writing a letter.

VLADILEN:

Dear you ten,

I'm coming home tomorrow. Yesterday I went for another
drive: Hollywood Boulevard, Sunset Boulevard, Mulholland
Drive. I stopped in Malibu. I have to say I was a little disap-
pointed. I was naïve. I thought everything was going to be as
shiny and beautiful as it is in language. But here it's only dull
reality, interminable rows of palm trees etc., strip malls upon
strip malls, etc. Also the sun flattens everything. The day be-
fore yesterday I climbed all the way to the observatory, where
James Dean runs into trouble in *Rebel Without a Cause*, not
very far from those famous white letters. I could almost feel
the breath of someone coming towards me, and the green or
almost blue or blue or almost green of his eyes, to try to start
up a conversation—as if it were enough to add sentences and
sentences to bring about a better world. And then a group
of children arrived to look at Saturn and Jupiter and Mars,
turning tirelessly around the sun, and everything broke up in
agitated chaos.

Peace,
Vladilen, the eleventh.

8.

A group. A conference room. Voices: Franck Projot, Aurélie, Coco, Myrtille. It doesn't really matter, since in general it's not clear who is who and who says what.

Oh I don't have anything against her, I swear. She's nice. She's funny. She's got a sense of humor.

Nothing against her but you're not for her either.

I'm with . . .

. . . Franck, Franck Projot . . .

. . . Oh sorry, Franck. I'm very bad with names, but faces . . .

. . . Still, she's a little . . .

. . . That's it.

Hello, sorry I'm late.

No worries, we haven't started yet. You're not even last.

Is there going to be a speech?

No just a moment of silence. The meeting got pushed back an hour.

So that's what "Silence Slot" means.

Oh I'm glad I'm not the only one. I've been wondering since I read the email.

No one's going to say even a few words, it's horrible.

I bet his religion means he can't.

Not even any lunch, and I skipped breakfast, thinking . . .

His religion means he can't?

Yeah I think so, I heard my boss's boss's boss saying. No one dies in their religion. God just raises them to glory or something idiotic like that.

I never did understand religion.

This is a secular enterprise, no religious conversations allowed. It's expressly stipulated in the Charter of Good Common Life.

Haven't read it.

Me either. Well, I saw that flirting with colleagues wasn't allowed and got depressed and stopped reading.

I don't understand how a *good* common life can come from articles and sections anyway.

Anyway what's going to happen to us? I mean worse than spending our lives in an office with a view of the parking lot.

You're new. The senior people look out on the city. And the very senior people have the park.

How long do you have to be here for the city.

It depends on how people leave. See, he's leaving a park so a city's going to move to park and a parking lot gets city.

But I just got here. You too right? Actually I don't even know your name.

Aurélie.

No flirting allowed.

I wonder if that Good Common Life thing is even legal.

It reminds me of monks. It's kind of like what they had. A charter like that.

Not at all. Monks lived in common but alone. They lived alone together.

You'll have noticed: when two people get close people are always suspicious.

Like sex was the only reason to get close to someone.

That's probably true, no, all the rest is just elegant trappings. We go into a meeting, we see who'd fit into the sexual position machine, and if there's someone . . .

Bingo!

I swear . . .

What?

Every morning in the train it's the first thing I do. I take stock of the people with whom it'd be possible.

Well anyway he's dead. A little respect.

"Silence Slot" hasn't started yet.

Somewhere I read that sexual excitement raises productivity at work. Well I don't know if I read it or made it up.

In Japan I can tell you: you'd never have these kinds of conversations at work. Never. In Japan, never.

Well in France not either, usually, especially in the symbolic presence of death.

In the symbolic presence? What, do you work in communications or what?

Well maybe you don't have them out loud.

But in your heart of hearts, inside . . .!

They're what, in Japan. I mean for religion. You have your own thing or . . .

A bell announces the beginning of the "Silence Slot." Everyone falls respectfully quiet.

9.

The clothed guy's apartment.

THE CLOTHED GUY: Sleep well?

THE BARE-CHESTED GUY: Great. What time is it?

THE CLOTHED GUY: 5pm. You told me not to wake you up.

THE BARE-CHESTED GUY: Yes yes. I dreamed that I was an architect and I was building a housing project. Not a big block but lots of little houses. It was called Peaceful Hills and the birds never stopped singing.

THE CLOTHED GUY: That was me. I was listening to a CD of birdsong.

THE BARE-CHESTED GUY: I see. They make CDs of that?

THE CLOTHED GUY: Yes and then when I go hiking I stretch out on the forest floor and I recognize them.

THE BARE-CHESTED GUY: They don't give a damn if you recognize them, if you want to know what I think.

THE CLOTHED GUY: So what was happening in your housing project?

THE BARE-CHESTED GUY: Nothing at all. It was really disappointing because I built it and no one came to live there. It was totally a desert, except for the animals. I handed out fliers in the subway. I hung posters, but it was a total desert.

THE CLOTHED GUY: Do you want something to drink?

THE BARE-CHESTED GUY: Thanks but I should go, my girlfriend's waiting for me.

THE CLOTHED GUY: I left some money on your jacket.

THE BARE-CHESTED GUY: Next time if you show me your student ID I'll give you a discount. (Taking his phone from his pocket and reading a message) Shit . . . she's already at the Front.

THE CLOTHED GUY: You're fighting at the Front?

THE BARE-CHESTED GUY: It's really Riccardo, my friend. I'm following him. Well he's sort of an ex-friend. My life's complete mess. Be honest: are you satisfied with the state of the world?

THE CLOTHED GUY: No but not to the point of struggle. I think first I've got to figure out how to change my life.

THE BARE-CHESTED GUY: Your life. That's your problem. Your life doesn't exist. Your life isn't yours but it belongs to everyone you meet. We've seen each other three times so .001% of your life belongs to me and .001% of my life belongs to you. What's called love is just when the percentages shoot up. Do you get it?

THE CLOTHED GUY: Yes. It's . . . it's . . . *(Trying to find the words)* That's what Riccardo says?

THE BARE-CHESTED GUY: Idiot. I have to go. The next time, if there is a next time—I'd like there to be a next time—I have something to tell you, ciao, goodnight.

10.

Three co-workers on their coffee break.

MYRTILLE: There's something I want to tell you but you have to promise not to repeat it.

FRANCK PROJOT: You know, that type of promise . . .

MYRTILLE: Yes but promise. The rest is up to you.

FRANCK PROJOT: I promise.

AURÉLIE: I promise.

MYRTILLE: Paul—Paul who's dead—asked me out to dinner three weeks ago. He said, you don't have anything to be scared of. I'm sick. I'm Paul who's almost dead and I don't want to exercise any kind of *droit du seigneur*. Even if I wanted to I couldn't, he said. The restaurant exuded luxury. Each table had its own little patch of artificial grass. You could control the noises you wanted and I put on frogs and cello. He said, I just wanted to tell you a memory so that the memory doesn't die with me. I said, you don't have anyone closer? He said, exactly. I don't want anyone to remember me, I want . . . I would like, he said, I would like, excuse me, I'm being rude, *I would like* you to remember only the memory. I said, why me? I thought he was going to say, your name, your smile, the shape of your ass. He said, because I've observed you in meetings and have noticed how precisely you remember things. We drank such delicate wine. You could make the lights how you wanted. I put on the warm planing light of the end of summer days. You could control the speed of the wind and the kinds of smells. I ordered steak and . . .

AURÉLIE: What smell did you put on?

MYRTILLE: I was going to put elm plus freshly cut grass. He said, wouldn't you prefer it to be random? I said, no put what you want. He put on sunscreen and hot bodies. I ordered steak and for the first time in my life I understood the expression "to melt in your mouth." When I was ready, when my memory was the most open, I said, and your memory? He smiled and said, my father listened to jazz all day long while he was working and fixing things or relaxing or playing sports. I couldn't stand that syrupy saxophone anymore. I felt like a goose being fattened up with jazz. I said, you didn't revolt, though. He said, no, exactly. Every time I felt like I'd had enough and was about to, there was that moment: my father just paused everything, "Stand still, you ever moving spheres of heaven . . ."

FRANCK PROJOT: ". . . that time may cease, and midnight never come . . ."

MYRTILLE: . . . my father would pause everything, and he would say, listen to this solo. He'd be in heaven. I said to myself, so there are people capable of such fullness they can just float up in a bubble like you go up in an airplane. That's happiness. I didn't feel I had the right to burst that bubble. I was never angry enough at him. He said, there, that's the memory. He smiled. He said, another bottle? I said yes please.

AURÉLIE: I'm so relieved. I thought you were going to tell us you had cancer.

FRANCK PROJOT: That restaurant must have cost a fortune. I could never take you there.

MYRTILLE: You don't have the right to ask me out to dinner anyway. Article 21, section 4.

11.

The couple from the car. Now they're in their bedroom, reading in bed. Outside the open window is a vast field of streetlamps—their house must be on a hillside—and the noise of cars coming up from town.

SHE: Listen. "Paradise implies the house . . . God created Adam and Eve so that they might keep each other company and talk with one another: but also with Him when He 'walked in the garden in the cool of the day.' House: counter-solitude, from God's point of view."

HE: That seems beautiful. Is it for your conference?

SHE: Yes.

HE: When do you leave for Boston, again?

SHE: In two days. My parents are coming to take care of the boys. They'll go trout fishing.

HE: Yes, you told me. Did you remind them that Marc's nineteen now? When you're in Boston, can you go see something for me?

SHE: Yes.

HE: It's where I stayed the first time I went to the US, to learn English. At someone's house, 37 Chestnut Street.

SHE: I'll go. Are you still in contact with them?

HE: No, but I am with the neighbors. You know, Seth.

SHE: Seth from Occupy Wall Street?

HE: Seth from Occupy Wall Street. He was learning French. As soon as he realized I was there, he invited me over to talk. He thought I was going to teach him something about Fourier.

SHE: Fourier of the phalanxes?

HE: Fourier of the phalanxes.

SHE: But you weren't really interested, except he had a very pretty sister.

HE: I was sixteen. No, he had two brothers. On the other hand, he was sixteen like me and he knew Fourier. The only Fourier I knew was someone I did judo with.

SHE: Wait. *(Turning the pages of her book)* "All written utopias have been social: an attempt to fix upon the ideal organization of power. Personally, I've often regretted the fact that there hasn't been, I've often felt the desire to write, a domestic utopia: an ideal (happy) manner of figuring, of anticipating the subject's optimum relation to affect."

HE: They included me right away. I was one of theirs immediately. It was like we'd had the same childhood. As if I'd always known the rules of baseball or had always slept in those same sheets, with leaping dolphins and whales spouting water. They didn't treat me like a stranger but a member of their own family.

SHE: You ended up exchanging clothes.

HE: Yes. How did you know?

SHE: Because I imagine you growing up and being afraid of becoming a lost body. I mean a single solitary body. You wanted to live inside the fiction that you still only had one body, only times four. So you exchanged clothes and you didn't wash them, and that made just one smell. At least by nose you couldn't be picked out individually.

HE: You've got me! You win. Such imagination.

SHE: But you haven't lost, either, because frankly your story's right out of a storybook.

HE: Sure but I'm offering you the win. Take it.

SHE: Then it's 8–5, me. Two more points and you have to give me whatever I want.

12.

A woman at her desk. Around her, the characters from her novel.

THE WRITER: In the novel I'm writing, the storm seems like it really wants to arrive. It's dying to start. A group of young people run to take shelter beneath a corrugated metal roof. The rain comes. Rain everywhere, instantly making rivers on the ground, which form deltas.

MANON: We could play a game,

THE WRITER: says Manon, five minutes later, opening a chocolate bar. She breaks apart the squares and passes them out.

AMINE: A game where all you have to do to keep playing is to play ─something that happens over time, like being survivors on a raft.

MANON: If this keeps up,

THE WRITER: says Manon, who looks at the sky, which is not letting up at all, not lightening anywhere,

MANON: Because it looks like it's going to keep this up.

AMINE: We're floating through time on this raft. The animals seem tame and watch us from the welcoming banks. We spin through rapids in the gentle water like in a water park. Like

HÉLENE: Shit!

THE WRITER: says Hélène, because the gutter's just collapsed on her. Soaked, she undresses, wrings out her clothes, and dries her hair. Everyone covers her with a piece of their own clothing. It's not cold and not frightening. These are the new storms of global warming.

CLÉMENT: The game I'm Thinking Of?

VLADILEN: In Indonesian, one kid is anak and more kids are anak-anak. Ngala boeah means to pick fruit by yourself. Ngalara boeah to pick fruit with other people.

AURÉLIE: We could pick raspberries, all of us. We could make jam, then eat the jam, memories of today in every spoonful.

HÉLÈNE: New definition of jam: preserved time.

CLÉMENT: In Indonesian, first person singular is "he" or "she." Third person singular is "I." Imagine a world in which I am the third person, never the first.

THE WRITER: Clément and Vladilen had traveled across Indonesia together the summer before. In Jakarta, whites and westerners and Christians or people from Christiandom party in shopping malls surrounded by electrified fencing. The cars go through explosive detectors before they enter.

AURÉLIE: In Jakarta, where men and women dancing can't touch either, they come towards each other, moving their hips delicately, and then retreat. Then advance. Then retreat. If the women are prostitutes, you have to give them a dollar bill each time.

THE WRITER: Aurélie wasn't on the trip but Vladilen told her. Vladilen taught her to dance that dance and now they all dance beneath the roof of corrugated metal vibrating in the storm. While advancing-retreating Mélissa says,

MÉLISSA: People think that sailboats are pushed by the wind. But it's actually the opposite: the wind accumulates on one side of the sail and creates a vacuum on the other side, and the sailboat advances to fill it.

MANON: Because sailboats are like everything else. They're afraid of loss. What are you afraid of?

THE WRITER: Manon asks Vladilen, with whom she is dancing. Vladilen makes an advance-retreat then answers her like he's holding out a dollar.

VLADILEN: I'm afraid of nights where I dream I'm not sleeping and the whole of the dream is the whole of the night I'm not sleeping and it's interminable.

MANON: Because it's night and because it's loss.

AMINE: Since we're all together on the raft, there's nothing to be afraid of. In Indonesian, sugar is *gula* and candy is *gula-gula*, I think.

HÉLÈNE: I think maybe I found a house for our squat. I didn't want to say anything yet because I'm superstitious. I'm going to keep an eye on it for two or three weeks, and then I'll take you there to see it. It's really big, just right for us I think. Very quiet. We'll finally be able to live together. Maybe. Meanwhile I think you should keep looking too. I'll know in three weeks.

CLÉMENT: Where is it?

HÉLÈNE: I'm not saying anything else. I'm superstitious.

13.

A man at his computer.

AMINE:

Dear you ten,

Just a note to tell you what I saw this evening: the dazzling colors of fruits and vegetables on the shelves, the bicyclist whistling and making little gentle zigzags like the day had promised him to something, the seamstress bent over her hems behind the shop window, the sign "Does A Job As An Electrician Turn You On?", the over-perfumed man in his quest after happiness, beer flooding into the raspberry dusk, the doors of the school open and playground being hosed down because it's Friday evening or maybe because the fleas have taken over.

Baci tutti,
Amine, the eleventh.

14.

A sex site. Two men and a trans woman. Only two of them are going to have an affair.

1 to 2: Hi.

2 to 1: Hi, what's up?

1 to 2: Good and you? Looking for?

2 to 1: Tenderness or fun. Up for anything

Seeking big cock for deep throat. Destroy my tonsils!

1 to 2: Cool. Me too. You're cute

2 to 1: Thanks. You too

Secking big cock for deep throat. Destroy my tonsils!

Small cock. Good luck

1 to 2: What do you do?

2 to 1: Med student

Up the ass?

Hi

1 to 2: Florist

Of course

Sry not my thing

Hi

2 to 1: Nice. Send me some flowers?

Boyfriend and I seeking tough bottom for double penetration

Hi handsome

Hi sexy, nudes?

1 to 2: Anything for you. Are you good with flowers?

Open

Blushing emoji

Never but tempted

2 to 1: I know roses and
actually I don't know anything

Amazing ass. Can I put my tongue

A shy sentimental one! A nice change.

Very sexy. Japanese trans woman here. My name is Coco.

You're really open?

Yes but very shy and sentimental, almost silly

I'm only top

Yeah top but flexible

1 to 2: No big deal, I'll teach you

Oh me too, a little! I think silliness has a cute side. Wink emoji

A top has the right to get rimmed

How many fingers

Surgery?

Quiet?

Yeah but your beard, must hurt

No. I don't want to.

User has left the conversation

Three fingers usually

You're really moaning?

When are you free?

2 to 1: What do you suggest?

1 to 2: Since you're fundamentally nice, I propose: I do what you want me to do to you. I love licking necks and ears.

2 to 1: That works, I love that too, thumbs up emoji, all the way to the shoulder slash armpit ^^

1 to 2: Mmmm totally

2 to 1: Plus biceps but then you have to take my shirt off wink emoji

1 to 2: I'll take it off. Or the other way around

2 to 1: The order doesn't matter since both put exclamation marks

1 to 2: Good plan. And lick your bellybutton?

1 to 2: Haha I don't think anyone's ever done that, show me, double wink emoji

1 to 2: Haha where were you raised?

2 to 1: I dunno but not that badly but still you can make it better. Wink emoji

1 to 2: I'm Tanguy

2 to 1: Mark, nice to meet you

1 to 2: What are you doing this morning?

2 to 1: I was supposed to go to the library but I can't make myself

2 to 1: What do you study?

2 to 1: Medicine exclamation mark

1 to 2: Oh yeah sorry you already said that. Anyway it's reassuring

2 to 1: Haha yes of course

1 to 2: Anyway I'm already reassured smiley face emoji

2 to 1: Haha good start

1 to 2: I love the beginning but when does the rest start?

2 to 1: When could it start for you?

1 to 1: Oh tomorrow exclamation mark

2 to 1: Not tonight? smiley face emoji

1 to 2: Theoretically yes. But I don't know what time I get off work

2 to 1: If you're ok with it I could invite myself to come sleep at your place haha. I like to spend the night it's nicer wink emoji

1 to 2: Ok with me four exclamation marks

2 to 1: Good start continues wink emoji

1 to 2: Yes. If it could always continue to start like this

2 to 1: Eternal beginning exclamation mark

15.

Two women, sixty or seventy years old. An ordinary street, ugly and pretty at the same time.

THE WOMAN IN THE PINK JACKET: Have you noticed? The shutters are open! They're finally back from their safari.

THE WOMAN IN THE BLUE CARDIGAN: Not so fast. It's not them. It's some squatters. I called the city about it.

THE WOMAN IN THE PINK JACKET: Oh I thought . . . I had thought . . . I was thinking . . . They were such a lovely couple. They'd take me to do errands with them. They carried my bottles of water. I wonder what happened, if they were planning not to come back.

THE WOMAN IN THE BLUE CARDIGAN: If they were lying when they said two weeks. You never know. The police down there, if you ask me . . . you can't count on anything.

THE WOMAN IN THE PINK JACKET: I so would have loved to believe that . . . *(Searching)*

THE WOMAN IN THE BLUE CARDIGAN: I saw a video on YouTube. (She pronounces it like your grandmother would.) A man in a zoo falls into the tiger pit. The tiger catches him like he's just a little mouse and woosh! He's dragged off easily into the thicket. Bye, man in the zoo. I'll send you the link.

THE WOMAN IN THE PINK JACKET: Are there tigers in Africa?

THE WOMAN IN THE BLUE CARDIGAN: No but they have lions, panthers I guess, cheetahs, leopards, lynxes, and monkeys who probably want revenge. Since we're more successful.

16.

The clothed guy's apartment.

THE BARE-CHESTED GUY: Is this a bad time?

THE CLOTHED GUY: No.

THE BARE-CHESTED GUY: Can I come in?

THE CLOTHED GUY: Sure.

(In keeping with his name, the bare-chested guy immediately takes off his shirt.)

THE CLOTHED GUY: You seem upset. Where are you coming from?

THE BARE-CHESTED GUY: A protest.

THE CLOTHED GUY: Again. Against what?

THE BARE-CHESTED GUY: Against the waste of perishable food.

THE CLOTHED GUY: Has it gotten worse?

THE BARE-CHESTED GUY: No. But it's gotten worse for me. I yelled with the others and then I stopped yelling and I thought: what, exactly, am I doing to increase the amount of goodness in the world?

THE CLOTHED GUY: And what did you tell yourself?

THE BARE-CHESTED GUY: Well yes I'm doing things, I'll explain. Soon. But not enough. I asked myself to whom I could give myself, for free, and here you are.

THE CLOTHED GUY: That's nice but I just jerked off.

THE BARE-CHESTED GUY: I could just hold you in my arms.

THE CLOTHED GUY: For free?

THE BARE-CHESTED GUY: Yes for free. The Bare-Chested Guy does that. Close your eyes. It could be for hours if you want.

THE CLOTHED GUY: I didn't even know there was a protest.

THE BARE-CHESTED GUY: Of course not, that's obvious. You're always here, with the blinds half-shut. The refugees, for example. You don't give a shit.

THE CLOTHED GUY: No I don't not give a shit. Well, I think, deeply and maybe honestly, yes. All that leaves me a bit cold.

THE BARE-CHESTED GUY. I heard someone in the subway say, "Oh the refugees, once you've seen one you've seen them all." It's terrible.

THE CLOTHED GUY: Funny, too. Very cynical but very funny.

THE BARE-CHESTED GUY: Are you really saying you're that selfish? You're truly not interested in anything?

THE CLOTHED GUY: No, I am! I want to know exactly where the light is when you wake up in the morning and the smell of your bedroom, if you have summer pajamas and winter pajamas, how many cups of coffee you drink and at what moment you slide your hand through your hair to smooth it down, maybe in front of the mirror in the hallway?

THE BARE-CHESTED GUY: That's very limited. But I'm flattered.

THE CLOTHED GUY: I feel protected in here. We go out in the streets sometimes but we're surrounded immediately. I feel like the littlest cat could jump right in my face and claw my eyes out. I barely even go to campus anymore.

THE BARE-CHESTED GUY: If you want we could go out together. I'll re-teach you the outside. Outside it's not all dangerous. The cats won't scratch your eyes out. Cats rub against your legs and sit on you where it hurts to heal you in their way. And you'll help me contribute to the improvement of the world.

THE CLOTHED GUY: What's your name?

THE BARE-CHESTED GUY: *(Slight hesitation)* Dylan.

THE CLOTHED GUY: No really, what's your name?

THE BARE-CHESTED GUY: Kevin.

17.

A hotel room, while she's cleaning it.

THE HOUSEKEEPER: I'm leaving. I left. I was already gone. Kevin is gone and Riccardo isn't coming. Kevin could have not left and Riccardo could have come. The sun rises every morning but now maybe it's evening. The sun is rising so it's necessarily morning. Kevin will come. Kevin is going to come. Kevin's coming. Kevin is here. Was here. Kevin was here and I didn't even say hello. You lost your bag. You lost your time, you waited for nothing. You lost time, you could have come quicker. Wait for me. Wait for us. We are happy to see you, royal we, old and old-fashioned. I wish that + subjunctive. Kevin has brought me my bag: would that he had. I will clean = certainly I will clean. I would clean = I would clean if. Note, however, that if you pay me to do it I will clean. Will. The salary at the end of the month comes. I don't think so. I don't think that the salary at the end of the month will come. Everything was better before it did not come. Everything was better after it came. Kevin forgot (once) to reimburse me. Kevin would forget (regularly) to reimburse me. In what epoch will you be happy? I don't know what to tell you, I don't know the answer. It's a mystery. Let's leave. Let's leave together. Let's leave in concert, hand in hand, in lockstep, in unison. Surely the people will revolt = it is not certain that they will revolt. The people will revolt, there's no doubt = the riots are already being planned.

The timer rings.

18.

Somewhere. The couple from the sex site.

TANGUY (Voice 1): Sorry I couldn't. I can explain.

MARC (Voice 2): Why?

TANGUY: I'm dying to make love to you. But not now.

MARC: You'd rather the beginning continue to begin?

TANGUY: I'm afraid that if we did it you'd disappear.

MARC: And you don't want to? That's adorable. Don't move.

The couple stays fixed in this position for a long time.

19.

A woman at her computer.

VÉRA:

Dear you ten, dear Clément especially,

I have this memory I can't shake. I'm going to tell it to you.
I have the secret hope that it might be like that little bit of
scotch tape in the picture book my mother used to read to
me, long ago, in once upon a time so long ago, at night so that
I'd go to sleep, so that there wouldn't be any ghosts, the bit
of scotch tape would stick to somebody else's elbow. Yours,
Clément? I'm on the balcony, above evening rush hour
traffic. The truth is that I'm waiting for a text that should say
"yes" or "on my way" or "of course." As the wait gets longer
and the suspense of the text intensifies, I'm overcome by an
anxiety I don't know how to calm, since I don't smoke and
I don't drink. I try to get my spirit to sit down all zen and
cross-legged in the interior of my body, which is hard. The
neighborhood church bells ringing help me along. That's
the memory. The memory where I wait endlessly to be
surrounded, but very peacefully surrounded, like a Russian
nesting doll, ideally packed inside another.

I love you all,
Véra, the eleventh.

20.

The street with the squatters.

THE WOMAN IN THE BLUE CARDIGAN: The squatters are still there! Incredible. I already called the city three times. No response! It's like yelling at a brick wall. You should call too.

THE WOMAN IN THE PINK JACKET: They're not mean or anything, you know.

THE WOMAN IN THE BLUE CARDIGAN: Well I won't be voting for that mayor again. Did you speak to them?

THE WOMAN IN THE PINK JACKET: They asked me if I needed anything. I said, you can help me carry in the bottles of water. I can't do that anymore.

THE WOMAN IN THE BLUE CARDIGAN: You let them into your house? What if they just decided not to leave?

THE WOMAN IN THE PINK JACKET: They came in and left. They offered to help me repaint the walls. I told them, my pension is ridiculous. I don't have enough money to pay you. I don't even have enough money to buy paint. They said, we'll do it for free. They said they'd steal the paint.

THE WOMAN IN THE BLUE CARDIGAN: They'll rip you off, watch out.

THE WOMAN IN THE PINK JACKET: They're young, they're dreamers. They're just experimenting.

THE WOMAN IN THE BLUE CARDIGAN: Stealing? You talk like we've been waiting for them.

THE WOMAN IN THE PINK JACKET: It doesn't move you at all?

THE WOMAN IN THE BLUE CARDIGAN: As Jacques Chirac would say—back when your protégés were still in diapers—roughly, I don't give a fuck.

THE WOMAN IN THE PINK JACKET: When you're young you can dream. Then time passes and you realize: no, not us either. Not enough strength or courage or determination or patience. Suddenly we're daydreaming, not dreaming.

THE WOMAN IN THE BLUE CARDIGAN: Personally I wouldn't give up a single one of my daydreams now for my old dreams. I had dreams—don't go thinking—like everyone else—it's genetic—oh I had so many dreams. Huge, grandiose dreams. But they weren't really about me. My daydreams are. I know who they concern: me. Straight to the point. It works every time.

THE WOMAN IN THE PINK JACKET: And you daydream about . . .?

THE WOMAN IN THE BLUE CARDIGAN: *(She hesitates)* It's a little . . . it's personal . . . private . . . I mean . . . well . . . you know . . . all of a sudden . . . in the street. Come have tea, this afternoon. We'll see.

21.

A woman at her desk. Around her, the characters from her novel.

THE WRITER: In the novel I'm writing, Véra with the immense eyes bangs her fist on the table and says,

VÉRA: If I have to kill someone I will.

HÉLÈNE: No surprise there. You always did want all the credit.

THE WRITER: . . . Hélène shoots back. The two are rivals. They've known each other for a long time, maybe since childhood, then lost touch. Incompatible temperaments. Clément intervenes.

CLÉMENT: Anyway we're not at that point yet, and if we could just avoid going to such extremes . . .

VÉRA *(interrupting him)*: Here it's the men who are cowards.

THE WRITER: Of course the incompatibility between the two women gets more complicated because Véra suspects that Clément prefers Hélène to her. In this novel, it's really just a secondary plot, but in a previous scene Véra admitted this to Vladilen.

VÉRA: Even if I just see him, all of me starts shaking. I think I need to lighten up a little bit.

VLADILEN: Do you think he knows?

VÉRA: I think he guesses. I want you to scope it out for me. I don't want to embarrass him again, even more.

VLADILEN: What if he doesn't know? What if he's thinking of someone else or no one else, or if he's totally wrapped up in our plans?

THE WRITER: In fact the heart of this book is the story of a collective. A group of sweetly elated young people have taken over a house and are planning a major action. They don't yet know what. Down with god, long live Us is the collective's provisional title. There are 11 of them. Véra weighs Vladilen's objections.

VÉRA: Anyway, try to find out where he stands.

THE WRITER: Now it's evening. It's the time of evening when the planing light gives everything an excessive golden thickness. Vladilen moves closer to Clément, who is looking meditatively at the grapevines and the humans' efforts.

VLADILEN: Are you not happy?

CLÉMENT: I am if I think about the old days, the road taken and the way I was with calm things calmly existing. If I think about the vineyards and the wine, the wasps and the stones, the griminess of people after work in the evenings, the noise of motors coming through the silence. I am if I think that there's only that world and that it's entirely enough, then I'm happy.

VLADILEN: But what about us, you're not happy about that? Have we let you down?

CLÉMENT: I'm an eleventh of you. I am one of us. If I was disappointed in you I'd be disappointed in myself too. Sit down.

THE WRITER: Vladilen looks for a stump to sit down on. While looking, he forgets Véra's request completely.

VLADILEN: This is maybe the time of day I like best, when the sun is going away and the smells start to come up from the ground. The cicadas slip out and the women call out "dinnertime!" to the kids who don't want to come in. You remember in Godard's film, *Contempt*...

THE WRITER: Vladilen, Amine, Manon, and Clément would met at the cinemathèque where they all used diligently to go.

VLADILEN: I'm against TV series. I don't know why yet but I'm fervently against them.

AMINE: I'm a generation late. I've always been. When I was born, I felt like I'd been a mole for twenty years, looking desperately for the uterus exit. My first cry in the light of day: I can't even tell you. Apparently I even burst the doctor's eardrum. I've loved opera ever since.

THE WRITER: This type of stupid sentence and overblown story had instantly brought them together—as it happened, one day, that age at which you're still afraid of being a solitary body and you need so much to belong to the litter. And now there they were, in that house and on that evening.

VLADILEN: You remember, in Godard's *Contempt*, the producer looks at the footage of Bardot as a mermaid, naked in the water. He laughs his big fat pig laugh and he says, "Gods, I like gods, I know exactly"—

MANON: "—exactly how they feel."

THE WRITER: finishes Manon, who is perhaps exactly a mermaid, coming up behind them.

CLÉMENT: The nymph coming out of the woods.

VLADILEN: The naiad coming out of the water.

MANON: Am I bothering you? Can I join you? Anyway I was walking, just enjoying the evening air. I was trying to put my ideas together. I wanted to go ATV-ing on the public ATV grounds but the tires were flat. I don't remember who said "gods last as long as the things they make," but the god of the ATVs is going to have to be repaired.

CLÉMENT: Sit down.

MANON: Continue.

THE WRITER: Vladilen smiles. The clouds are that Tiepolo pink, the sun shining through them from behind.

VLADILDEN: It might seem vulgar when the producer laughs at the mermaid. You can hear him hearing the money come pouring in. But they're cries of joy, and he's letting it out because he's taking the side of the gods planted in the garden, the pagan side of the presence of the real world, real light, real things. He's the only one who still hears the mermaids singing and this fills him with a happiness that means he has to grunt. So that's why I'm going to propose that we call our group The Mermaid.

MANON: The Merman, I'd rather say. Not maid.

CLÉMENT: Or how about The Mer-people, in the plural.

22.

In the company cafeteria, a secluded corner.

MYRTILLE: I thought about your proposition, Franck. I think we can use first names now. I'm ok with it.

FRANCK PROJOT: Not yet, because 1) it's almost more romantic these days, if not, and 2) better than no one suspects anything here.

MYRTILLE: But I can't have anyone over. My boyfriend's sister lives in my building. That's how I met him, anyway that's the truth. It'll have to be at your place. Not at a hotel. Hotel decoration dissolves all my desire—I mean, as far as hotels that fall within the limits of my budget go.

FRANCK PROJOT: Did they hire a new chef? This food is almost edible. I don't live alone.

MYRTILLE: You have a girlfriend?

FRANCK PROJOT: I live with ten others in a house we're squatting in. I don't have my own room. But I can probably find a free one, no problem.

MYRTILLE: Whose house is it?

FRANCK PROJOT: A couple's. They left on safari and never came back.

MYRTILLE: Are they dead?

FRANCK PROJOT: We don't know. Maybe they came upon some ivory traffickers who killed them and left their bodies out in the open air for the hyenas and vultures to gorge themselves on.

MYRTILLE: And there are really eleven of you, living together. Collectively, really?

FRANCK PROJOT: We're friends who live together according to an ordinary and general freedom.

MYRTILLE: I don't think I understand.

FRANCK PROJOT: We try—slowly, patiently—to increase the intensity of freedom. In the squat there's no boss but there are no collective decisions either. Besides, we try to make it so that there are as few decisions as possible.

MYRTILLE: I'm not quite sure I've completely understood yet but you can explain again sometime. And you don't have your own room?

FRANCK PROJOT: Not to myself. But I'm telling you, if there's someone there no one will come in. We have freedom of use.

MYRTILLE: How many bedrooms are there?

FRANCK PROJOT: Seven.

MYRTILLE: The couple had a giant house.

FRANCK PROJOT: Inherited, I think. They were the last of the family.

MYRTILLE: Your system can't be very practical for the sheets.

FRANCK PROJOT: We sleep in each others' sheets. For example, if one night the sheets are too dirty or stale, and I can't sleep, I change them. I wash them. That's my responsibility.

MYRTILLE: Uh. How about you wash them before I come. I'm not a wimp, not totally a wimp, but still . . .

FRANCK PROJOT: That might be hard. I don't know what room's going to be free then. You can take some time to think about it, you know. But the idea is that we own nothing, not our bodies or even or smells.

MYRTILLE: Okay, I'll think about it. I think.

23.

A woman at her computer.

COCO:

Dear you ten,

I'm at home. There's no one. Where are you? I'm waiting.
I thought about posting my patience on our wall. When I
come back home, when I hide out in our little living room,
behind the curtains, in the room with our one table, when in
the kitchen I eat penne with scallops and leeks that someone
cooked for at least four of us—but where did you ever man-
age to steal scallops?—when I'm not waiting anymore, when I
get out a sweater and a shawl to wear, when I am so alone and
so calm, in the light of a single lamp, when I feel your faces
inside my face, when I hear our names calling to each other,
when—when we make a dwelling in the evening air, a shelter
made of leaves, where living there together is enough, and so
I keep repeating the same poem to myself—
If you want to hear it, press like.

xoxo,
Coco, the eleventh

24.

The woman in the blue cardigan joins the woman in the pink jacket, who is sitting on a park bench in front of the squatters' house.

THE WOMAN IN THE BLUE CARDIGAN: You were sitting here when I came by this morning.

THE WOMAN IN THE PINK JACKET: Yes, I'm thinking. Véra taught me part of a poem.

THE WOMAN IN THE BLUE CARDIGAN: Who's Véra? Don't tell me she's, I don't know, one of those women? From the house. Is she?

THE WOMAN IN THE PINK JACKET: "Even if the lights go out; even if someone tells me 'That's all,' I'll sit here anyway. One can always watch."

THE WOMAN IN THE BLUE CARDIGAN: And you've been taking that literally since this morning? Bravo!

THE WOMAN IN THE PINK JACKET: I noticed that the stones over there between the trees and the metal restrooms are in the shade the whole day. Tomorrow I'm going to borrow a wheelbarrow and move them into the sun, because it isn't fair that they don't get any.

THE WOMAN IN THE BLUE CARDIGAN: That's very nice of you.

THE WOMAN IN THE PINK JACKET: Yes.

THE WOMAN IN THE BLUE CARDIGAN: But maybe those stones prefer the shade. Maybe they're stones equipped with a chemical structure that the sun erodes. Do you know anything about what the stones actually want? If

I were deaf and dumb and blind and paralyzed and you said to me, "I'm going to put you in the sun," I'd scream on the inside: "I beg you no I beg you." Well, probably in slightly stronger language than that.

THE WOMAN IN THE PINK JACKET: You're right. I'm speaking for the will of the stones.

THE WOMAN IN THE BLUE CARDIGAN: Will you introduce me to your new friends?

THE WOMAN IN THE PINK JACKET: So you can make fun of them?

THE WOMAN IN THE BLUE CARDIGAN: I promise not to. It's just that nothing ever really happens here. And you do seem happier than before. As happy as you've been since your husband died. I'm jealous.

THE WOMAN IN THE PINK JACKET: You see, the world can change.

THE WOMAN IN THE BLUE CARDIGAN: I never said it couldn't change. I said that no one knows how to make it change and we shouldn't try.

THE WOMAN IN THE PINK JACKET: The first lover you ever had—did you let him sit down beside you, without doing anything?

THE WOMAN IN THE BLUE CARDIGAN: Yes, I didn't look at him. I let him press against me.

THE WOMAN IN THE PINK JACKET: You didn't make a single sign that could have let him know whether he could or he should or whether it was imperative that he continue.

THE WOMAN IN THE BLUE CARDIGAN: I was silent.

I was incapacitated. I worried that the slightest gesture might be the wrong gesture. I even kept my lips hermetically sealed in case my breath disgusted him.

THE WOMAN IN THE PINK JACKET: You've never moved in your life?

THE WOMAN IN THE BLUE CARDIGAN: Never.

25.

The couple from the sex site, somewhere, starts moving again.

MARC: Oh this is nice.

TANGUY: Next time I'll come to your house.

MARC: I don't think so. I'd have to tell my mother that I like men and what's more that I like men her husband's age.

TANGUY: Isn't that your father?

MARC: Yes.

TANGUY: Ok. Is your name really Marc or is it Marc-Antoine?

MARC: Just Marc.

TANGUY: But what nineteen-year-old guy is called just Marc these days?

MARC: My parents are nuts. They even changed our last name. Before it was Estienne. Now it's Comestor. Marc Comestor. Like Pierre Comestor, you know?

TANGUY: I'm a florist. Mostly I know the names and the lives of plants. I know that Lenin seriously wondered whether a professional revolutionary could love flowers and the response was nope, forbidden.

MARC: Ok, but do you know Comestor?

TANGUY: No.

MARC: Comestor means who eats. As in, comestible, etc. An academic from the Middle Ages who read so many books—all the time for all his life—that the others nicknamed him Comestor, as in devourer. Ideal for my parents, who spend their lives in bed reading.

TANGUY: You think they'd react badly?

MARC: To my gerontophilia? I don't know. We just don't talk about it. My love life isn't a subject worth talking about. Do you meet people online often?

TANGUY: Some.

MARC: This is where you're supposed to say: "Yes often, but not like you."

TANGUY: Sorry. I'm bad at compliments. It's true, I've never slept with someone who's 6'6".

MARC: You don't really notice 6'6" in bed. I thought florists were better than other people at creating illusions. Do you make bouquets or just sell flowers?

TANGUY: I make bouquets. I try to sense exactly what someone wants to say to someone else, and I choose flowers, stem lengths, shapes of leaves, arrays of smells. I calibrate the colors. I want the bouquet to say one precise thing.

MARC: You should put up a sign: Florist-Therapist. What's the most beautiful thing someone's ever told you?

TANGUY: First, are you not taking pictures because you think you'll always remember me? And, second, what you told me a little while ago.

MARC: What did I say?

TANGUY: You said, "Your eyes are shining." I said, "Why do you think." You said, "I don't know. Happiness? Joy?"

MARC: That's not a very beautiful thing.

TANGUY: Yes it is. Someone tells you, "Look, look, you're brimming with happiness." It's almost unheard of.

26.

The writer, her office and her characters.

THE WRITER: In the novel I'm writing, Hélène is in the kitchen. Out the window, in the park across the street, the light seems to liquefy the trees—if that makes any sense. Hélène is making coffee for anyone who wants it. She's wearing headphones. It's a tacit rule here that if you want to listen to music you wear headphones. No one needed to decree it because rules come about naturally in their common life.

AMINE: . . . by spontaneous generation.

THE WRITER: . . . Amine had said, one night when the eleven were discussing the organization of the house.

AMINE: The rules of our game must be born though spontaneous generation.

VÉRA: What does that mean?

AMINE: Every time you cook something, if you make enough for at least another person, even if the house is empty, even if it means you just put it in the fridge. If everyone does that and also feels bound to do it, then it becomes a silent rule. No one decrees it. Our life together suggests it.

CLÉMENT: Fine with me. Except for the word "game."

HÉLÈNE: Right, it's not a game.

MANON: It's not a game. It's a proposition of world.

THE WRITER: But Amine, who was very beautiful and—what's more—a Winnicottian (Donald Winnicott, 1896-1971)—didn't get flustered. He waited until Kevin had handed around the beers he'd just gone to steal . . .

AMINE: It's just that you're not taking the game seriously. Winnicott says that to control what's around you, you have to *do* things, not simply think or desire, but *do things*. Winnicott says that to play is one of the best ways of doing this. Winnicott says that play stems from asking what makes a life worth living.

THE WRITER: Now Hélène is playing. She is arranging a pyramid of glasses. Out the window, the two old women have on their gardening gloves and are watering the garden. Are they playing too? Hélène thinks. She thinks,

HÉLÈNE: Is it possible to be old? Yes it's possible. Is it possible to be old and to play the game "I hope"? Yes it's possible. It's possible to be old and to close your eyes, and to imagine hearing the floor creak, and the noises near you, and suddenly the whole world is bending towards you, and there are arms holding you, and you still belong. Is it possible at any age to open the door and say, "Now I'm going, now I'm gone, it's morning, it's whatever time and it's also morning, the cool freshness, the delicious rush-hour dust?" Yes, I imagine it's possible.

THE WRITER: The pyramid continues to rise—the squatters' house contains an enormous number of glasses—and when it falls Kevin comes running.

KEVIN: It's ok. Don't worry. I'll help you.

HÉLÈNE: Thanks. I don't know what came over me.

KEVIN: No big deal.

VLADILEN: Can I help?

THE WRITER: . . . says Vladilen, who also heard the racket in spite of his headphones.

KEVIN: Because we're all here, I was thinking, I'd like to introduce someone . . . for the twelfth.

VLADILEN: Who?

KEVIN: One of my clients.

HÉLÈNE: You want to bring him here out of love? You can't bring people here just out of love. Véra and I had to un-love Clément.

THE WRITER: That was true. They had fallen out of love with him.

KEVIN: It's a client. I'm not gay. I'm going out with the housekeeper, for now, at least for now.

VLADILEN: So what qualifies him as one of us?

KEVIN: I don't really know how to say it. He's a recluse. He's not interested in anything but the details of the world. There are only details, he says, only details. When he's touched, caressed, it's like bouncing on a trampoline. I mean, that's how much he responds, with all his being. I feel like he'd take root very quickly if we transplanted him here.

VLADILEN: You're saying it's a little like he's the past we're missing.

KEVIN: Yes, a little like that.

VLADILEN: We'll put him in a pot and he'll become the long history of this place.

KEVIN: That's it. The leafy, exuberant past.

HÉLÈNE: Our past. Welcome, past.

27.

An office. Soulless, shabby furniture. Manon in her paid role as employee of the federal administration.

MANON, THE GOVERNMENT EMPLOYEE: I told him, "Come in. Sit down on this chair. The other's wobbly, the usual administrative misery you'd expect. How are you. We are here together today to help you re-orient your existence."

THE ORDINARY CITIZEN: I smiled, playing the part of the cool and calm individual. I said, "Thanks. How're you? Your bay window is magnificent."

THE GOVERNMENT EMPLOYEE: This was the strategy of 87% of the population: the smile of someone who just happened to be here, otherwise everything was fine. I said to him, "We'll have to find some good questions to ask you. Please excuse me for getting straight to the point, but you've seen the line in waiting room. Do you know the good questions?"

THE ORDINARY CITIZEN: I smiled even more openly. I knew she was thinking I was like 87% of the population, a bad actor, hypocritically cool and calm. I took off my jacket slowly. "I have all the time in the world," my slowness proclaimed. I raised my arms so that she could see the halos of sweat dampening my shirt and I felt her body contract. I folded my jacket before placing it on the wobbly chair.

THE GOVERNMENT EMPLOYEE: I thought, he's more clever than previously anticipated. He's brought out his animal sweat. Did he spend ten minutes running around the block just before the meeting to warm up, preparing to leap straight at my heart? I played the silly girl suddenly electrified. I clenched all my muscles up on purpose and in my best trembling voice I said, "Do you know the way? Are you on the right side of the hill?"

THE ORDINARY CITIZEN: When she started talking about hills I started to doubt. The question was too rationally strange. I knew she was playing at being disconcerted but in truth she was facing it directly. Immediately I changed my strategy. "I don't know if I know the good questions," I said.

THE GOVERNMENT EMPLOYEE: Was it that he had abruptly changed strategies or was he really lost? "What would be your questions," I said.

THE ORDINARY CITIZEN: Will we go to the movies together? To the theater? Or simply out into the night and the spectacle of nature and the stars we share?

THE GOVERNMENT EMPLOYEE: I think I stared at him with my mouth open.

THE ORDINARY CITIZEN: She stared at me with her mouth open. I saw her crooked overlapping teeth and that she had bitten her tongue.

THE GOVERNMENT EMPLOYEE: Is that really a real question? Instinctively I closed the portals of sensation. A professional reflex, fortunately. It crossed my mind that he was a federal inspector testing my affective disengagement capacities and that, satisfied with my performance, he would give me a rating that would lead to a promotion that would lead to 300 more dollars per month immediately.

THE ORDINARY CITIZEN: I felt her sudden fear that I wasn't who I seemed, but a trap, a snare, the end of her career. She drew back—like a sea anemone who's touched the crab's famished claw—I mean, if crabs eat sea anemones. I should check that.

THE GOVERNMENT EMPLOYEE: I said to him, "Now you know everything. Think about it and come back and see me." I wanted him to hide those halos under his arms.

THE ORDINARY CITIZEN: I knew there would be no further meetings. I could feel it. She was going to pass my file on to one of her colleagues. I got up. I said, "How many questions, waiting without response in the infinite space of questions, are there still to ask you? That's a question," I said.

THE GOVERNMENT EMPLOYEE: I looked him in the eye, I was trying to come up with a response that could potentially knot his intestines with that certain anxiety of the hunter before his possibly consenting prey.

THE ORDINARY CITIZEN: She said, "Questions are different from calls." I felt my mouth go dry.

THE GOVERNMENT EMPLOYEE: He said, "Could someone murmuring your name serve as a solution?"

THE ORDINARY CITIZEN: I said, "Are humans capable of making questions so tricky, so prickly, so hard, that they're insurmountable?"

THE GOVERNMENT EMPLOYEE: My heat was beating with happiness, like a hungry cat who has just crossed a field full of brambles and to whom is given, out of pity, a handful of Friskies.

28.

Myrtille and Franck Projot in the company cafeteria.

MYRTILLE: I thought about it. I'm going to pass this time.
I can't see myself making love in some stranger's sheets.

FRANCK PROJOT: You could bring your own sheets with you.

MYRTILLE: They'd smell like sex. My boyfriend would
smell that they smell like sex and demand an explanation.

FRANCK PROJOT: We'd wash them. There's a washer and
dryer in the house. The electricity hasn't been cut. They
were paying by month. They were the last of their families.
No one declared their deaths. Maybe they're not even dead.
Maybe they're living out a perfect love in an isolated hut on
the savanna or maybe they were kidnapped and enslaved.
We have excellent blueberry jam. There's a creaky wooden
staircase. There's a hammock big enough for two hanging
in the attic. There are these miraculous beanbag chairs that
mold to the exact shape of your body. There are voice-control
lights. There's dust that falls tranquilly all around us.

MYRTILLE: The sheets would smell like a different deter-
gent than ours. How could I explain that to him?

FRANCK PROJOT: We could go by the store on the way.
We'd steal the exact same brand of detergent, the same
scent. Forest Pine with a hint of lemon.

MYRTILLE: You're that desperate, or is it really me?

FRANCK PROJOT: I know you'd love the view from the
attic, the trellises, the hollyhocks. Everything is elegant and
gracious. There's a winter garden-library. There's wax that's
been there for decades. The house gives everyone the feeling
that childhood's ahead again, a second childhood, a childhood

full of irresponsibility and perpetual games, like a childhood should be. There are ghosts who grab you suddenly by the heart, maybe, if you believe in them, if you want to believe in the consolation of ghosts. There's that dust of the world in which we could leave our traces.

MYRTILLE: Next week?

29.

A cell. Coco recites poems by Takuboku Ishikawa in Japanese and then improvises an English translation. If there is no Japanese-speaking actor, ordinary poems may be chosen from any language spoken by any of the actors.

A POEM: In the tramway there was someone
Who spit
Even that gave me pain.

A POEM: One day
I changed the paper over my windows
And my heart got lighter.

A POEM: Like a telephone would call into the distance
Today still that sound in my ear
Sad day.

A POEM: My next day off
I'll spend it sleeping.
I've been thinking of this for three years.

A POEM: Nothing is happening
I'm gaining weight easily
Definitely I miss something.

The housekeeper is thrown into the cell.

COCO: Hello. What's landed you in here?

THE HOUSEKEEPER: In the movies they always say that the detainees don't wonder why they're there.

COCO: You think we're being filmed.

The housekeeper looks around her, then gleefully points towards the top left corner of the room.

THE HOUSEKEEPER: Yes, there.

COCO: Ok. My name is Coco. I get guys on the Internet. I find the richest men, and I go to their houses, and they eat my pussy that I've carefully coated with sedative in advance. Then I steal whatever I can.

THE HOUSEKEEPER: How did you get caught?

COCO: A guy was drinking ginger juice. I think he had a dry mouth or something. Minuscule salivary glands. It diluted the sedative. He woke up in the middle.

THE HOUSEKEEPER: I steal from the guests at the hotel where I work.

COCO: That's not super smart.

THE HOUSEKEEPER: You don't know me. Maybe I want to end up in prison. I started when Kevin said, I'm going, I'm gone, forget me.

COCO: Who's Kevin?

THE HOUSEKEEPER: He said, I'm leaving. I'm going to live with the eleven. You're keeping me from being one of them. Not you in particular, anyone would.

COCO *(suddenly understanding Kevin's affair with the housekeeper)*: Oh. I see. He said, I'm sorry. He got that irresistible teddy bear look that makes you want to forgive everything pronto.

THE HOUSEKEEPER: Yes exactly. How did you know? He got that look and he said, I'm sorry. Truly, heartbroken. Forgive me. Or not. Ok now I'm leaving. Now I'm gone.

COCO: From now on. Forever. Already and always.

THE HOUSEKEEPER: Even if I weren't leaving I'd shrivel up so small you wouldn't even see me anymore.

COCO: He said, farewell.

THE HOUSEKEEPER: Good luck.

COCO: I wish you a brave life.

THE HOUSEKEEPER: Exemplary.

COCO: Don't ever get raped.

THE HOUSEKEEPER: Not if possible. Is someone going to bail you out?

COCO: Bail happens in the movies. Not in our little lives.

Tanguy of the lovers is pushed into the cell. He doesn't look at the women, or he does.

TANGUY OF THE LOVERS: Listen, I'm sorry. I love you. It's probably neither the horizon of your anticipation nor the domain of your expectation. It happened unexpectedly. One day, on a beach, the clouds gather quicker than expected and the rain proves positively diluvian. Same in the mountains. The locals always warn us, but regularly we forget to listen. I love you and now something's missing. Like going down a long slide and the pool never arrives. There's never the warm collective water in which we were supposed to explode with happiness. I know. I only saw you once. It's a little crazy. But I remember that we stayed huddled together for seven hours, like barnacles against their rocks. Your back was full of light, you would've thought there were electric lightbulbs inside. You covered me methodically in your saliva, like a snail. We listened to our respective pulses beating at the ends of our fingertips. I exploded with happiness. I felt complete proximity, for once nowhere else except in proximity. I am not immature. I did note our wild egocentrism. I know that in your system, I'm a very distinct planet orbiting your own solar reality. Or let's say Pluto, which has been demoted. It's not even a planet anymore but a trans-Neptunian object, a single and solitary object, but also one of a good thousand trans-Neptunian objects. But it doesn't matter. I love you. I have proof, like waiting for your few texts with misplaced and sickly impatience. Please, I want in again. Go off camping for three days. Come back smelling like muck, frozen feet, unable to distinguish your socks from your skin. I'll take care of everything. I'll peel your socks off carefully in hot water. Just get me out of this prison where I'm kept in exile, exterior to the interior. Please release me back out of the world where it's possible to go everywhere.

30.

The reading couple, in some boulders.

SHE: We should have followed the path.

HE: That's true, but we can't retrace our steps. The sea's rising. We have to keep going this way.

SHE: You're the one who wanted to go through the boulders.

HE: You're the one who wanted to take a walk.

SHE: You're the one who said this morning at breakfast with your mouth full of crunchy buckwheat toast, "Anyway if it's nice out we should do something."

HE: You're the one who went online and found this island where we were supposed to be enjoying the saline brightness of life.

SHE: Excuse me but I love the anxiolytic lapping of the waves. The aluminum smell of the sea.

HE: We can't go any farther. We can just sit on this rock and wait.

SHE: Let's hope the tidal coefficient is weak. What's going to happen to the boys?

HE: They'll continue to live for a while and then they'll die, like everyone, forever.

SHE: I shouldn't have been such a snob and pretended like I wasn't interested in their private lives. I should have asked Marc if I was right in thinking that he likes men.

HE: We should have made Justin promise never, and I mean never, to convert to monotheism.

SHE: Not even Buddha.

HE. Especially not Buddha. Off limits.

SHE: The sea's rising. We should stand up. My feet are wet. It's going to stop, knock on wood. There's no wood here, but I'm knocking on the knotted wood of my teenage desk. I got A's in everything.

HE: We've said the least about our third child, Séverin. We never know what to say about Séverin.

SHE: You forgot, he's raising spiders. He knows everything there is to know about insects. He's already figured out the exact path of his future professional orientation.

HE: Our children are not spending their lives playing video games. We don't have those types of kids. That's a success.

SHE: They're not listening to Beyoncé or whoever it is they're listening to these days.

HE: I thought you didn't want to be such a snob. But you're right. Death to pop music!

SHE: Death to pop culture!

HE: Death!

SHE: The water's up to my knees. I'm thinking of everyone who ever said that death doesn't matter.

HE: "Death arrives; it would be a thing to dread, if it could remain with you. But death must either not come at all, or else must come and pass away." Seneca.

SHE: More.

HE: "Epicurean doctrine depends on the idea that the disarray of the individual leads to the loss of feelings and, on the other hand, based on this conclusion that whoever is deprived of feelings has no importance for us." Cicero.

SHE: I knew I could trust you until the very end. When I saw you for the first time, in the entryway, with the sun slanting sideways over the house, making the red tiles explode with light, the first word that came to mind was: unwavering.

HE: You're not getting too cold in this water? Now it's up to our hips.

SHE: And later, in the meadow, with the breeze and the sweet blowing grasses, I thought: unwavering. I'm cold and I'm scared.

HE: Once I fell from a galloping horse. It was on an island, like this one. A herd of horses came up behind me with the jolting noises of their hooves. I did the opposite of what I thought I would do. I closed my eyes and thought, whatever happens, happens. Adieu. Adieu, my fleeting organization of atoms. I didn't look death in the face.

SHE: I forgive you. Weakness is human. Put your hands on my breasts and stop my heart from being so cold in this wintry ocean water.

HE: So it's true: we're going to die.

SHE: Adieu to the two cats, the teapot and the herbal tea, to the new microwave we never used.

HE: The boys will use it. An ideal tool for adolescents suddenly deprived of parents.

SHE: Well then I'm not sorry we bought it. It even weighs things, their density, the proportion of water in them, and it calculates the ideal time it emits waves. Do you think they'll know how to make it work?

HE: They'll know. We've had an ideal life. We did our best.

SHE: We've perfected each other, as much as possible. Hold me tight. I'm numb and panicky.

HE: I've still got a square of salted chocolate in my left pants pocket. What irony!

SHE: Chocolate with sea salt! My mouth is watering. I wanted to come up with something to tell you. Something that would abolish regret.

HE: I thought the regret was the juicy hearts of red and yellow summer berries.

SHE: The exploding heart of the tomato. Shit, it's everywhere. I'll have to change my t-shirt.

HE: Don't worry. Just don't die. Don't die. But now you're dead and heavy in my arms. I'm going to have to leave you. Will the mermaids let us drift the waves together, if I beg them? Forgive me. My muscles are seizing up in this icy seawater. I'm letting you go.

She falls back on the bed. He falls on top of her. They make love with unusual ardor.

31.

The clothed guy's apartment.

KEVIN (THE BARE-CHESTED GUY): Are you done packing?

THE CLOTHED GUY: I don't feel like taking much. *(Tapping his forehead)* Everything is here. Are you sure that the eleven are going to want me?

KEVIN: Yes. Well, the ten. I already want you.

THE CLOTHED GUY: How are you so sure?

KEVIN: I've always been very intuitive. I promise.

THE CLOTHED GUY: *(looking out the window)* It's raining.

KEVIN: That's true.

THE CLOTHED GUY: It's not fair, when you think about it.

KEVIN: What?

THE CLOTHED GUY: If I say, "it's raining," you can go to the window and say, "it's true, it's raining," or, "it's not true, it's not raining." But if you say, "I promise," I don't have any way to refute that.

KEVIN: Later you'll be able to confirm it. The promised world will be realized. Or not.

THE CLOTHED GUY: But you won't have lied. You'll just have been wrong.

KEVIN: Well, anyway, the promised world will come true. Don't worry.

THE CLOTHED GUY: Usually that never happens. Unemployment is supposed to go down and it doesn't. The plumber is supposed to come and he doesn't.

KEVIN: In some countries, the plumbers arrive on time.

THE CLOTHED GUY: In this country, the country in which we live, people are not dependable. Plumbers of course, but not just them. Artisans in general, people in general, unemployment in general.

KEVIN: Where we're going to is sort of an extra-territorial space.

THE CLOTHED GUY: Am I going to need my passport?

KEVIN: I have it here. *(Tapping his pocket)*

THE CLOTHED GUY: What color is the promise?

KEVIN: Brick red. Garden overflowing with flowers of all kinds. Two old ladies take care of the plants. They're so gifted you could say they have fluorescent green thumbs.

THE CLOTHED GUY: And, say, does fear disappear as soon as I enter the living room?

KEVIN: Yes.

THE CLOTHED GUY: Ok, andiamo.

But the clothed guy hesitates, stops.

THE CLOTHED GUY: Are you really going to live up to my expectations?

KEVIN: Not only me, but we, the eleven together. We've re-exalted the most disappointed revolutionaries so that you won't be disappointed. We've consoled humiliated men and women. We've re-inflated the morale of troops at the edge of defeat.

THE CLOTHED GUY: Really?

KEVIN: In a manner of speaking.

THE CLOTHED GUY: But what have you really done that could fill me with pleasure?

KEVIN: Nothing. We do nothing but we do it gently, with infinite tenderness, to accelerate the healing of the world.

THE CLOTHED GUY: Crazy, that's what I told you the first time we met. That I wanted to put an indestructible protective coating around things. Do you remember?

KEVIN: I've been thinking of you for the twelfth since the first day we met.

THE CLOTHED GUY: Ok. Let's go.

But the clothed guy hesitates, stops.

THE CLOTHED GUY: You know, it's better to let me believe that I'll get there eventually.

32.

A man at his computer.

CLÉMENT:

Dear you ten, maybe eleven,

It's night. I'm waiting for all your regular breaths, except for
Coco and Kevin who are working the market for sex at this
hour, when levels of solitude in the streets are the highest.
I wanted to explain something to you. If we're in the coun-
try and I say, that tree, it has to be the tree at the end of my
pointing finger. If I say, a truck, okay. But if I say *this* truck
and you say which—you look everywhere and there's no
truck, there are only hills and vineyards and the smell of the
earth and muskrats, and Vladilen stretched out on the ground
breathing it all in intensely, then we're in the country. You're
probably thinking that I'm hallucinating, I must have taken
something. That's what I'm trying to explain. It's called a
deictic. A deictic is a word that has no meaning beyond its sit-
uation. We talk. We talk in order to find the exact right words
for our present situation, like the hydrangeas who love shade
and humidity and abound with happiness against the glare
of granite. Here and nowhere else. Especially me. I talk too
much and I'm tired. Maybe I'm just babbling. I'm the most
talkative of all of us. Fortunately each and every one of you,
in turn, approaches me and scores my body, and my child's
fear—the fear that provokes language—seeps out and runs
like the sap of an injured tree. If I say I love you, anyone can
be "I" and anyone can be "you." They're just the feelings we
animate between us.

When I say "us" I'm thinking of us,

Goodnight, goodnight, goodnight,
Clément, the eleventh, maybe the twelfth

33.

In the squatters' garden, now luxuriant

THE WOMAN IN THE BLUE CARDIGAN: We're in the garden. Thank you, all of you.

THE WOMAN IN THE PINK JACKET: Without you, I'm not sure I would've found my way. Don't thank me. This is our collaboration.

THE WOMAN IN THE BLUE CARDIGAN: Our co-operation.

THE WOMAN IN THE PINK JACKET: Look. Here we have some Mabel Morrison roses, with their unruly flowers. And then the Georg Arends, whose petals fold into sharp corners.

THE WOMAN IN THE BLUE CARDIGAN: There are blue irises.

THE WOMAN IN THE PINK JACKET: Over there, the aromatics, which used to be called simples. Thyme bay laurel rosemary basil mint chives parsley burdock I forget what else.

THE WOMAN IN THE BLUE CARDIGAN: There are withered daffodils. I planted them because of a poem I learned by heart in school: "A poet could not but be gay / In such a jocund company." Gay in the old sense, of course, from our childhood.

THE WOMAN IN THE PINK JACKET: Joyful.

THE WOMAN IN THE BLUE CARDIGAN: Laughter like clear mountain streams.

THE WOMAN IN THE PINK JACKET: My mother used to drag me to church. She'd drag me like an enormous unwilling parcel, but she was strong as a plow. Even so, there was Psalm #133 All I remember is Ecce quam bonum et quam iucundum habitare fratres in unum. Behold how good and how pleasant it is for brethren to dwell together in unity.

THE WOMAN IN THE BLUE CARDIGAN: And a weeping willow, because of the tent of coolness it makes on suffocating summer afternoons.

THE WOMAN IN THE PINK JACKET: Can a willow give shelter from the wind?

THE WOMAN IN THE BLUE CARDIGAN: We'll try.

THE WOMAN IN THE PINK JACKET: There are cherry trees loaded with fruit, like a sudden uncontrollable emotion after a wait.

THE WOMAN IN THE BLUE CARDIGAN: There's dew in the mornings.

THE WOMAN IN THE PINK JACKET: There's sainfoin.

THE WOMAN IN THE BLUE CARDIGAN: There's catnip.

THE WOMAN IN THE PINK JACKET: Indian paintbrush.

THE WOMAN IN THE BLUE CARDIGAN: Even a bench. Come sit down.

THE WOMAN IN THE PINK JACKET: I scattered snails everywhere.

THE WOAMN IN THE BLUE CARDIGAN: One day, in a country house, with my husband's friends—my second husband's—it had just rained buckets. I went out I stepped on snails with every step. Tiny little snails in shells that didn't resist at all.

THE WOMAN IN THE PINK JACKET: But not these. They came here too.

THE WOMAN IN THE BLUE CARDIGAN: Here it's immanence itself, here in the world itself, even.

THE WOMAN IN THE PINK JACKET: Over there, all the way over there—actually quite far—I planted barley, corn, wheat, spelt, rye, buckwheat, quinoa, rice, manioc, and tapioca.

THE WOMAN IN THE BLUE CARDIGAN: And here, within arm's reach, like a sheltering rim around us, the humidity of the ferns, the bamboo, the cane. Perhaps all childhood to come is held here, simply hidden at the feet of the ferns.

THE WOMAN N THE PINK JACKET: In the little bamboo huts.

THE WOMAN IN THE BLUE CARDIGAN: In wicker hideouts.

THE WOMAN IN THE PINK JACKET: And there, all sorts of mushrooms. "And these roses, all these roses . . .

THE WOMAN IN THE BLUE CARDIGAN . . . on which, from a cloudless sky . . .

THE WOMAN IN THE PINK JACKET: . . . a magical snow fell, one summer's day."

THE WOMAN IN THE BLUE CARDIGAN: A phenomenon explained by the winds at the highest levels of the atmosphere.

THE WOMAN IN THE PINK JACKET: The garden.

THE WOMAN IN THE BLUE CARDIGAN: The garden, finally.

THE WOMAN IN THE PINK JACKET: First we'll populate it with birds. What do you think?

They go off, crossing the stage into the world they made.

34.

Inside the house.

CLÉMENT: Do we have something like a theory of the world?

VÉRA: Something that would give it back in its abundance—as abundant as a river on the day of a flood warning.

AMINE: Sometimes you hear people say, I do my best, I live the only way I can. Does our theory make the human "only way I can" any easier?

MANON: I saw a man on the train take off his jacket and make a discreet phone call, and I thought that that was enough. The first step on our Richter scale of happiness.

AMINE: The human "please" as in "please, save me."

HÉLÈNE: Is it possible to solve an equation with n number of variables if you only know one thing, that the result has to be positive, generously positive? Yes, probably.

AURÉLIE: I saw a man trying to find something in his back pockets. He had glasses. If I had asked him for his name I would be able to tell it to you, maybe. One fewer unknown person.

VLADILEN: I brought a cat into the house. I asked if anyone was allergic.

AURÉLIE: I'm allergic but I'll get over it.

VLADILEN: He sleeps for 22 out of 24 hours. That's a lot, even for a cat. And then I thought, if he always sleeps outside, maybe he's permanently half-asleep, sleeping in danger, of course—but here, in our fortress—

FRANCK PROJOT: We're going to have to decide when to vote on the twelfth joining us. If he should participate in our assemblies.

HÉLÈNE: So far, with the patience of a saint, he's seeking sweetness in the winter garden.

CLÉMENT: Or maybe not a vote. A cooption would be more natural. Tomorrow, I propose we count the number of smiles he provokes in us.

COCO: You're sure it's not out of love?

AMINE: Climb with me onto the raft. Finally you're up on it with me. Thank you for following me. We float. Don't abandon me. Let's swim. Thanks for still following me.

KEVIN: I simply let his head fall onto my chest. I let him come onto my chest and rest there like some kind of bird. And we remained that way, simply embracing, a tree in a park. That tree down there protected by green barriers so that the children don't climb into the branches and fall. Best scenario broken arm. Absolute worst total paralysis, lawsuit, trial, city goes bankrupt, local taxes rise considerably, etc. Is that a definition of love?

MÉLISSA: The man I was telling you about, on the train, was wearing blue pants. Blue like you see sometimes on tarps over the backs of trucks.

MANON: Let loose the dogs, I thought, looking at his pants, let loose the dogs, let them devour me.

MÉLISSA: I'm not especially afraid of death. I'm afraid of being dead when I die. I don't know if you understand the difference. I'm afraid of being immobile and silent and alone and solitary and isolated and forsaken.

COCO: I stole some books from a guy's house. Tons of books. They're outside in a giant truck. I was thinking we should build a library. Cardboard shelves, very chic. Perfectly recyclable, fair trade.

VÉRA: I was thinking we should build a gym: a machine for the right abdominals, another for the obliques, another for the transverse abdominals, another for the pyramidalis. And a treadmill. I thought, to run until you're exhausted and to sleep before the sadness of the evening.

MÉLISSA: I always think, what if they forget to bury me with a sweater.

HÉLÈNE: Does one of your books say, "Live together in order to be able to stand the sadness of the evening?"

COCO: I don't know.

VÉRA: Surely one of the books says that.

FRANCK PROJOT: One of the books says, on page ninety-five, "I don't want a life that grates all day long. What I need is a quiet life, a life with no noise." End of quotation. What is necessary, my friends, is to make sure the floor is watertight, because problems are like floods. What gets you is the capillary action.

CLÉMENT: I'm pretty sure that one books says, "Oh, my friends, there are no friends."

AMINE: Please. Please.

KEVIN: I just let him come.

AURÉLIE: We have received a letter from the electric company. They're going to cut the electricity. There's no reason, they say, no logical reason you should be authorized to live for free.

III.

Three Sisters

LUCKY

—You can call me Lucky.

The boy grinned at her. Lucky, that's a pretty name. It's unique. The next question was always, And is that your real name? Lucky would answer, Not just Lucky. Lucky Prairie. If you're good, I'll tell you why. It never failed. The boy would say that he wanted to be good, what did he have to do to be good, etc. A well-oiled machine. It always worked. The next morning, at least, Lucky had somebody's warm skin to wake up against. Often, early, the boys would say, don't kiss me, my breath's like a hyena's, seeing how much they drank yesterday, but it didn't bother Lucky. She loved everything animal, everything that reminded her of the body she could have, supple and quick in pursuit of food or mating. And then getting up, a shower or not, together or not, coffee or tea. The uneasy passing moment. Are we going to see each other again? Do we want to see each other again? Lucky would say:

—Well, this is *real* awkward,

in her best all-American country girl accent. The boys who wanted to see her again, the ones after more of her know-how—her goosebumpy kisses behind the thighs, for example—would choose that moment to remind her that she still hadn't told them about her name. She responded:

—Next time.

The door shut.

Lucky wanted someone to rub her shoulders and to play with her hair for hours on end while explaining something serious about the fate of the world. What was missing was someone who could do that. Someone to explain—it didn't matter what the explanation was. Also he had to be good with his hands.

Lucky Prairie worked in a beauty salon in the center of Rennes. When asked what she did, she'd say:

—I'm the main employee at Planet Beauty.

—Main employee, meaning. . .?

Well, more like the boss but vaguer than that. It didn't really didn't fit anywhere in the standard hierarches. In fact, she worked hard and had earned the confidence of Lise, who was the owner and actually the boss. In her self-appointed role, Lucky reigned over the lives of the other employees with a severity that didn't make her very likable, but that was efficient enough so that Lise could be left in peace to do other things. For example, to collect plates. Also Lucky was beloved by her clients, who took her as seriously as she took her work to heart. She would bend over backwards and then some to attain—to consolidate—beauty. It's like I make the world younger in my own way, she would think.

When she got home, Lucky would listen to Peggy Lee's smooth "Johnny Guitar," humming the words in the shower. *Maybe you're cold but you're so warm inside.* While she hummed she turned the shower knob all the way towards hot as if she were beneath a heated waterfall and she was going to be enveloped in another body. She was drowning in another body. She was happy. She had decided that her own Johnny existed, somewhere, and that she would search for him every-where. She wanted her life to be like a romance novel. Why not? Why would she have wanted anything else? Besides, honestly, who in the world really wants anything else? Under her shower-waterfall, she dreamed and dreamed, striking the most striking poses she'd ever struck. Consequently her water bill was always extraordinary. This is exploitation, she said while she signed the check. But the song went: *I was always a fool for my Johnny.* She had proof of being foolish. This was necessary and perhaps sufficient.

She knew she'd be in love when a man didn't seem too stupid or too petty. She waited for a man the size of Johnny Guitar. When she got tired of waiting, she would go to the station and act like she was saying goodbye to someone. She chose a destination and a train. Then when it was time and the train was leaving, her heart broke and she cried hard. It was a good solution. If she was alone, it was only because the other person was somewhere else. Not nonexistent, just somewhere else, traveling. She invented lives in which she'd finally go join him. For example, Johnny had to leave for an entire year of fieldwork for his anthropology dissertation, and she'd just said goodbye and see you soon. Many of Johnny's fake lives had been borrowed from certain of her clients, and for this she was deeply grateful to them. She took much better care of those clients after that.

Once, at the station, while she was waiting for another train to leave, a very beautiful man sat down next to her. His black Adidas were torn. This meant he was poor, but nowhere did it say that Johnny couldn't be poor. He had on a white T-shirt and his eyes looked a little lost. He asked her for a cigarette and she said sorry, she didn't smoke. He turned to someone else without even a thanks anyway. But Johnny didn't have to be polite. In fact maybe that was just as well. Someone who wasn't polite might remember—better than anyone else—the animal in us who demands to be satisfied. And then he got up:
    —Excuse me.
    —Why excuse me?
    —I'm going to go smoke a little farther away. You don't smoke. Lucky marveled at the gesture. She asked him to stay there: sit, thanks for having thought of me but stay. Please stay. He looked at her with an expression that said: what does she want from me—or, does she want me. Lucky thought about it. If Johnny wasn't not polite but profoundly sensitive, what a miracle that would be. Then two policemen appeared, and it seemed like they knew the possible Johnny. They called him by name, checked his ID, and wanted to take him to the hospital so he could get better. Apparently he had smashed up everything at his mother's house. He was fever-ish and he didn't want to go. I only broke a table, he said, refusing. You don't have the right. And then the ambulance arrived. The female doctor had a very soft voice, sweet from years of studying compassion. The guy broke down in tears. For days, Lucky regretted not having intervened, because she would have been good at cradling him and letting him cry it out. Lucky felt she had some good cradling deep inside her

and that she needed to find a body—she called it a Johnny—
who had the same rhythm she did, or who could sense the
rhythm inside her.

She wanted a story to happen to her, but nothing ever came
about. What story could she tell?

To Lise, the actual boss, she had pitched the idea of opening
a men's department—facials, massage, exfoliation, manicures
and pedicures—but it didn't go over very well. I guess we're
still just in Rennes here, sighed Lucky, disappointed. What's
more, the few men who came were each one gayer than
the last. Not that that was a problem in itself, not at all, but
when she watched a man who wasn't watching her, Lucky
felt lost. Or it was like being sure of a path that led nowhere.
Or getting an email that had bounced back after three days:
UNKNOWN RECIPIENT. Her friends didn't understand
it. There are other things in life besides *that*.
    —Oh yeah? What else?
    —Well like your work. You always say that when you
clean up someone, make them up, you put order back into
their life, like you're a sort of body therapist. You always say
that, right? Lucky said that, and she believed it. But in her
own life, the only thing that could put anything in order or
make sense of things or open up a time that wasn't chaos was
that. One of her friends took offense.
    —So we don't count?
    She didn't feel like explaining and she wanted still less to
have to justify herself. She watched her friends with an air of
defiance and at the same time she looked like a cornered ani-
mal, a trembling hare. One of the friends came to the rescue.
    —Probably we all have our other things besides *that* in life.
Walking in nature, for example, said Eugénie, that's my there
are other things than that in life. For me it's my issue or at least
an issue. Lucky agreed. To each her issue, to each her means
of survival. Besides, she also liked walking in nature and
being prey to the elements. Or rather, being in the elements,
maltreated, contained, or enclosed. One stormy Sunday, she

hurried to the nearest beach. The grains of sand stung her legs and arms. Her lips were gritty with sand and the wind pushed in some impressive black clouds. At one point, she stopped to watch the wind erasing her footprints. Now she was on an island or it was like she was on an island. No one could have said how she got there. She was there, that was all, set down in the wind. Maybe someone dropped her off and was going to come back to get her. She would wait. She just had to be patient. Johnny would come, or he'd come back.

Lucky in the Parc du Thabor. She's waiting for something she could call her story to happen to her. She's sitting in the grass. The trees have the color and the density of a rainy summer. The lawns are damp. The mayor has installed trampolines for the kids. Lucky doesn't get tired of watching a shy, melancholy child who passes the afternoon jumping and jumping, making up the best of all possible worlds. When evening falls, and there isn't anyone to see or make fun of her, she goes to the trampoline to have for herself that moment when the imagination becomes so strong that it consoles completely. But she can't quite jump far or high enough. Or maybe consolation is inaccessible. Perhaps the brain chemistry of children leaves them a chance at it—but not us. After adolescence, maybe we can't just jump into our happiness anymore. But who knows why?

Or maybe she would have preferred another child, the blond kid with his legs folded beneath him while eats his crepe stuffed with blueberries and looks around curiously, because he doesn't understand what she wants. She doesn't understand what she wants either. A child like that, so blond, so cute, like bread dough you could handle, warm brioche, a delicious child-pastry. A bed where she could come and kiss and caress him until sleep came, or a man who could give her this type of malleable, edible child. But it should be noted that Lucky was thirty-three and soon thirty-four, and for her it was practically finished. Life took place somewhere else.

While she did the dishes that she'd let accumulate all week, Lucky wondered: how is it possible? She saw no reason to have a dishwasher for just her. How is it possible that life is already over? What is the structure of time? It's too late was one of the phrases she repeated most often. She'd repeated it since childhood. It was as if as soon as she arrived some-where—as soon as she fell madly in love for example—it was too late. The train had always just left and you could see the black smoke behind the curtain of trees, on the other side of the station. You could hear the locomotive's whistle, and imagine the train breaking into the distance, skimming along through plains scattered with bison, and Johnny at the window, his Winchester on his knees, asleep but barely, on his guard, invulnerable, etc. In fact it might be too late for this comparison, too. Anyway even the gesture of bidding farewell to someone with whom she was madly in love, she did belatedly. Lucky hadn't been lucky enough to live at the right speed, something like that. Changing her name and everything, it was all useless. She had summoned the minor goddess of luck, but luck doesn't so easily let itself be cajoled.

Alone, solitary, lonely, isolated. So many words to say almost the same thing—except not at all. The first is the simplest and it fits her best. I'm alone, she thought.

One night at the Sablier, Lucky met a man who was thir-ty-three and who had almost drowned that very afternoon, trying to save an eight-year-old child at the beach. Maybe he wasn't even eight. The child was swimming with a friend and a treacherous wave had swallowed them up, far from the shore. Actually not too far, but far enough so that the child lost his footing and was getting worn out paddling in the foamy tur-bulence. There was a point when the child's friend, who was ten or eleven, said: sir, please help, he can't do it anymore. But saving someone isn't so simple. Another incoming wave struck the man who was now holding the child with one arm. . .

—See, it sucks you down just like a toilet flushing (Lucky didn't love the comparison)—and now neither of them had any footing and they were both struggling against the undertow. The child latched onto the man with his arms and his moving gaze and the man reassured him as best he could but he was also tiring, out of breath in the waves—

—I promised myself, no more cigarettes if I made it out. Ultimately things ended well, thanks to the attending life-guards. But when I came back up onto the sand, the man said, I felt like throwing up and crying and my girlfriend said, go on, cry. Oh. Once again, Lucky had missed the wagon, like her mother always said. We missed the wagon. But so as to do something for him anyway—to take him into her arms in her way, to murmur to him that everything was and was going to be OK—she offered him two 50% off coupons for Planet Beauty.

—You can give them to your girlfriend if you don't want them.

And for the rest of the night, Lucky thought about the man. Specifically she thought, *When I was eight, no one saved me, and maybe that child would always feel saved, and what's the age limit for when if you haven't been saved once by then, you won't ever be?*

When she closed her eyes, sometimes Lucky saw a car bearing down on her. Quickly she opened her eyes to avoid an accident. She wondered why there was such intense traffic in her head and who, exactly, would want to kill her? The scene might repeat dozens of times. It didn't depend on how she stretched out in bed, on her stomach, on her back, in a fetal position. Nor on whether she closed the curtains or not or left the night light on. It didn't depend on her computer, with its loop of nature noises, running water, crashing waves, rain falling in the rainforest, nor on whether or not she put in her earplugs. After so many avoided accidents, she took the two little blue pills that led her out onto the prairies of sleep. There was no one anywhere in sight, and certainly no cars. Everything was silence, or rather there was only the noise of the grasses in the wind—and Johnny, who must be sleeping somewhere and would eventually get up.

Anyway, it was necessary for her to be desirable at every moment, so that if Johnny encountered her he'd recognize her. There are other things besides that in life doesn't mean life is reduced to pieces of skin and to tongues in mouths. It doesn't even mean what good would it do to renounce pleasure. It means we're bodies and it's the only way we live.

Of course Eugénie was right to say: when you walk in nature or in the fields, when you let the sun or the wind or the night rise up over you, then the world, too, bears witness to your existence. For example, one day they went sailing together, with Julien, Eugénie's boyfriend. They set off from Saint-Malo and Lucky spent the whole trip throwing up—it was a way of living, she told herself to be able to stand it—and then they dropped anchor at the Chausey Islands. In the morning, at dawn, Lucky got up and rowed to land and pulled the dinghy up on the beach. No one was up yet on the main island. She was truly solitary, alone with the paths, the fortress, the cliffs, the light. Or almost truly solitary: she was solitary, along with the gulls. She felt herself as the corporeal companion of something. She felt: I can truly, correctly, speak the word "now." She stretched out and fell asleep in the grass, beneath the cover of the trees, and the landscape made for her a Johnny who flickered in the light. It lasted a few minutes, not long. She went back for breakfast with her friends, in case they needed the dinghy or in case they wanted to return home with the tide.
    —There was such silence, she said.
    —But that's not silence, said Eugénie. Humans call it silence when there's no human sound, no sound that evokes our fellow men, no motors or voices or songs on the radio. But that's not silence. Humans call it silence when they have the impression of having left the species to enter into a better reality. No, not better, Eugénie corrected herself. An adjacent reality, vaster, more spread out, more enveloping, or maybe just different. But it isn't silence. Lucky and Julien agreed. According to Julien, real silence would drive us mad

with terror. Real silence would mean the world isn't there anymore, Eugénie confirmed. But what Lucky wanted to say was: despite everything, a landscape gives us only one choice, which is to dissolve into it. Was that the same thing as a Johnny? A Johnny who would conjure up my shape among the things? Who could make me a new form, a new identity? What if Johnny called me—would that be that my real name? But she didn't say anything. She listened to the water beat gently against the sailboat's shell. They decided to wait until low tide to go see the archipelago and to stay there for the rest of the day. In the afternoon, Lucky and Julien made love while Eugénie went jogging on the island, but it didn't have any consequences.

There are other things besides *that* in life means that it's not worth looking anywhere else. It's the only solution and the only peace. If I kiss someone's fingers, one by one, one by one the finger joints, even the scales of the nails, if I breathe into the palm, I help the person be born.

Lise proposed that Lucky buy Planet Beauty, because she wanted to go back to train seriously, in the old business—
    —The old what?
    —The old everything!—and Lucky thought she would probably accept. She scheduled a meeting with her banker. In any case, she thinks she prefers the business of the living.

Lucky thought that it was too late to have a story—really and truly a story. Besides, she suspected that no one ever really had a story. Instead life consists of tatters of things, scraps of narratives, scattered pieces. But nothing ever continues from A to B and B to C etc. etc. all the way up until you could calmly pronounce Z. Nothing coherent enough to become a story, properly speaking. One day, at the station, during the crush of the rush hour when she had gone to say goodbye once again to Johnny, by accident she bumped into someone who avoided a stronger collision by placing one hand against her torso and the other against her back and holding her. A nanosecond caught in the vise of his sweetness and then he was already making his way away. She watched him leave in the crowd at the same speed her own sensation was departing. But that doesn't mean, she thought to herself, that in a certain way you and I, we didn't make love deeply. *What if you stay, what if you go, I love you.* That was what the song said, and Lucky could back it up. She repeated it over and over—a little trick, a charm—in a very low voice because apparently she couldn't carry a tune.

After that, Lucky kept a notebook of all the sexual relations she had, visible and invisible. When he stretches his arm out, reaching across the table in the café for his cigarettes, a cloud of his sweat comes over us like an aphrodisiac fog. Our sexual relation. It's nice out, the shadows of the trees. His arm touches mine when he points out the place and the name of a theater. I feel the little ephemeral tickles of his blond hairs on my arm. In the park, crowds of boys playing soccer and basketball. Our own prairie.

BEATE

Beate, you're late, her friends said.

It was true. She made vague excuses, the subway was a mess. In fact she had come on foot, hence the lateness. It didn't matter. In the dim light of the bar, collapsing into the banquette's dark, plush, and probably dirty depths, she thought: I shouldn't have come. I should have stayed outside. Outside, the world was waiting for rain. It was very beautiful, every littlest thing waiting suspended for the arrival of the storm. A red-bearded waiter came to take her order. He was a good twenty years younger than she was, at least. What did she want? A long silence and then she said, oh, whatever you feel like making.

—A Black Russian?

—Sure. She didn't know what that was. Probably vodka and. . .? She let her gaze run along the sophisticated lines of flattering LED lights that adorned the ceiling. Probably there was some kind of new scientific algorithm for calibrating levels of light to optimal consumption of alcohol.

—I'll be right back, she said.

She sat down on the toilet and read the graffiti on the stall walls. It was one of her tricks for avoiding the obligations of friendship. She hid herself behind the locked door and imagined the lives behind the noises the other women were making in the neighboring stalls, their slowness or speed, the clicking of their bracelets, whether or not they wiped the seat. Not all the lives went with all the gestures. The only *I* was the one behind the door, reading and rereading the writing on the walls. THE NEW WAITER WITH THE RED BEARD IS A SLUT—and what, exactly, makes up my life?

Later the same evening, her friends introduced her to a man and immediately she stopped being mad at them. Besides, she didn't really know why she had been mad in the first place. Because they had deprived her of the storm that hadn't even started? She was sorry but she had to ask him to repeat his name, with the music and all, you know—

—Clément.

They talked about various things, like walking. She said: when I walk, and I walk a lot, sometimes for hours, on the weekends I like to take the train to wherever, I live alone, I'm single, I don't have kids, I'm moving out of my shoebox apartment, as soon as I see a path that leads up I want to take it, I always want to get to the highest place. It's not to feel on top of things, it's to—a pause—calm down, I think.

—Calm down from what?

—Up high, it just makes sense. I can see everything coming up towards me. Like they used to be able to from a fortress. Like just in case, I could always go hide.

He said that he also liked to walk, but she didn't know if he had just made that up to please her, even if he really did like to walk.

Everyone left because everyone had to work early the next day. She went to the waiter and proposed an astronomical sum if he'd go home with her. She didn't usually do this and she had really no idea what the going rate was. Of course he accepted. He wasn't really a waiter, he said, he was a free-lance producer. He would just have to wait until the end of his shift. THE NEW WAITER WITH THE RED BEARD IS A SLUT. After, later, when it was over, she explained him that she needed to re-prepare herself.

—Re-prepare yourself for what?

—For the tenderness of human gestures.

He wanted to know if he measured up, if he had re-pre-pared her. Actually he was a little upset. He had thought she desired him so much that she offered him that astronomical sum on the spot.

The next day, 8:55am, Clément texted her to wish her a good day at work. Already, she thought. It was a sign. She tried to be detached, a swallow, effervescent. She kept having flashes of memories, her husband. She went back into the kitchen and put her book down on the table. There was usually some utopia in the book, usually sentences celebrating each letter of the word, C-O-U-P-L-E. At the beginning, her husband would appear in the kitchen with the first noise, the first smell, like it was instinctual for him. At the beginning, they often made love there in the room where they first encountered each other, not even undressing, like they show in movies to signal uncontrollable desire. All the way to work, she and Clément carried on a very chaste text conversation. She opened her hand and out fell a cotton ball that had been stuck to her palm.

That same night they went to the movies. Obviously he had chosen the film for her. In it, someone sacrificed himself for someone, giving up his money and almost his life. It was a film for the feminine part of the population. Someone knocks; flowers; someone re-knocks; re-flowers. That sort of thing. She didn't like it. She preferred when soldiers have to run from tree to tree and dodge bullets and survive. As soon as they came out they went back in for another film, laughing. The other film was better. The soldiers had to take back some Pacific islands. Many of them perished but there was one in particular beneath the canopy of trees, an ideal old-fashioned hero surrounded by his fellow soldiers. The light came down in rays. His eyelids trembled. He was going to die. Someone caressed his forehead. He was going to die at any second. Someone said to him: find something that's yours to hold onto. At that moment Clément caught—caught, covered—her hand.

His hands: he wants to be able to disarm me. He wants know what spectacular animal's going to emerge from the den of my stomach, she thought.

—Beate, you've changed, they said to her at the bank where she worked. Have you got someone? Yes, maybe. Maybe because what would it mean to have someone? Is it enough to know his name? With a sudden onset of new confidence, she decided she would like to be the new union representative.

   The first walk with Clément was in the Bois de Vincennes. They sat down in the undergrowth. The sun filtered through the verdant sieve of April foliage. The fallen trunk was hard to sit on, but it was the first walk so anything was completely possible. She let herself go in his arms: as if I had fallen and someone picked me up, cleaned me off, warmed me up. She wasn't thinking of the insects, who were making a meal out of her, leaving horrible welts.

The second walk with Clément was in the Bois de Vincennes. It was raining, but they embraced beneath the imperfect cover of the leaves. They still got wet. Later she got a nasty cold that settled thickly in her mouth and throat.
　　—You shouldn't kiss me, I'm sick.
　　She kissed him and then buried her head in hair that smelled like almond shampoo.
　　The first time they took a walk together in real nature, they went by car to a little village. The May forest towered, the wheat was on the ear, an ancient abbey, the hems of their pants wet. They laughed. He took her by the hand and they were happy, at ease in the order of the landscape. They climbed up an embankment, as high as they could. The abbey's strong white architecture rose before them, making arcs and points in the sky. There was only the sky behind that, outrageous in its dark gingerbread undertones. They sat on a rock. She watched him thinking. Am I the final conclusion of his thoughts, the permanent result? She didn't dare ask, and anyway he was holding her hand, he drew her into the damp grass where they were even happier.

Some say that a hand caressing the skin sets off an electrical chain of neurons, and along with it the feeling of entering into interminable duration, something that can cross and outlast death. Not only.
　　Some say that a sex that swells, a sex full of veins, contains all the verbs with "come" in them: become, come from, come back, overcome. Not only.
　　Some say that to give head = delicately to cover all the lives that unfold on earth, the life of the worker-apprentice whose hands age fast, the life of the professional soccer

player, the life of the cashier who waits until 10 pm and runs fast for the 10:19 train, all the lives held in my mouth with care, attention, and compassion.

Not only. Some say that to be penetrated means crossing and knowing what happens beyond any border, becoming an alien, a foreigner who smiles inside, who might be able to build a shelter in the new country. Who might be able already to speak a new and better language, a language for conversation, for words that become acts. Temporarily realized utopias. Not only.

Each time she does it, she looks for a clue about why she wants to, why she only thinks about doing it, why she has no other ambition in life. Some say that to do it is to repeat the word "yes" of general reconciliation, an armistice of breath. Not only.

HIS WIFE (A PAINTING)

Her husband went out yesterday. He went to see the galleries, and then he came back. The same evening, he had explained to his wife why he hadn't been a painter. He talked about the color orange and the notion of boredom. His wife had had the impression she'd already heard it all, elsewhere, in another life, sitting in the middle of a sea of other faces, a birthday, was it a birthday? Someone had leaned over and said: do you need my fingers? She had opened her mouth and retrieved the bit of carrot stuck in her teeth. And then someone else who her friends had called Long Distance had sworn that he knew how to transform himself into photons and that he had moved himself over behind the lamp just by speaking the words. This, it seemed, was one of God's favorite tricks. She got herself another glass of punch instead.

That was in a periwinkle spring, with nights clear as water, when people repeated what others had already said, "I look at you and I would rather look at you than all the portraits in the world except possibly for the *Polish Rider*." She had responded by smiling a smile that took responsibility for all of futurism. Even then it wasn't every day that she managed to escape to the point of living in a world made magnificent by aesthetics itself. Then everyone had passed on again to something else, since to pass is the verb that best suits time.

—Listen, what time is is a sort of cross-dressing mannequin who gets you shitfaced while kicking you. And then you're old.

—That's surrealist, said a woman who had the voice of a poodle. Maybe she had been speaking of the way our bodies are the residues of ancient memories, or of all the bodies that we drag around on leashes.

It was a spring of alcohol and marijuana. There had been songs that everyone sang and bodies twisted and contorted themselves with the music, which began at a certain point to seem diabolical. At that moment, the dancers had stopped abruptly. She stayed still in her chair watching their disarray as they bumped against each other in their haste to flee sadness, down the stairs—and there, a new success: the discovery of a model for the ideal end.

But that spring had been some time ago already. The DVD spun and spun and it was the next morning. Her husband had abandoned her to the kitchens of solitude. And yet she felt a violent yearning for conversation. She wanted to talk about the climate and regret and the fields of change. Around her was the excitement of summer. She knew this because the windows demanded to be opened. Suddenly it was logical to go see something: a coastline, a monastery, a foundry. There were so many little trips to take. The fledgling birds were waiting, and the cherries growing calmly on their trees.

—Do you remember? said her husband, in her memory. She responded, yes. The paths, the dawn, the fluorescent green fields, the wet hems of their pants, a doll left in the grass, the whole gently rural landscape.

—Oh, but darling, you were thinking of the compresses of consolation.

Of course it was all made up, but living is also made up most of the time. It's enough to imagine a charming episode and to believe in it. There was the time they lost their glasses in the woods because someone had been explaining something fascinating. They were completely incapacitated. While they were looking in vain, between the ferns and the wild straw-berries, the sun shone down and still the old story carried on: I left, I don't know where or with whom and I no longer remem-ber from where I was coming but I understood at that moment that one day my face would no longer be with me.

And then it had come to pass. It was the summer we left our faces in the closet because no one really felt like wearing something so old and threadbare. Maybe we could still stand the lip-chin arrangement, or the appearance of breasts, but that was it. The rest had been erased, or, rather, it had been crumpled up and thrown out as if by a child who's messed up his red line and wants another blank sheet but here we are, sorry, completely out of stock. And yet I swear to you that we were stretched out in the grass and the world seemed

like it must have been infinite. It was simply so good to be
stretched out there, close to hope, in possession of the intu-
ition that someone was getting into the tram with the firm
intention of getting off at my stop and of running towards
me and telling me what was hidden in the bonsai tree of
his heart. It was the summer when, for absurd reasons, we
waited for a word that would release us, even the word—say,
"bog"—as empty as it is in any other language, but we had
lost the street map and no one spoke our dialect.

That evening—of course, another evening—her husband
had come home aching and out of breath, like he'd just run a
marathon or two. All day he had been selling relaxation sessions
to young executives with money and now there was the little
spot of the moon, shining like cream cheese. There was only a
melting star and the moon and her own breath and the blood-
less phantom of her husband stretched out on the couch. It was
the autumn when the names disappeared. People were eating
sandwiches on the steps of the temple that day at lunchtime, in
the heat that was slow to disappear, but it had become useless
to call out to them. It was useless and maybe counter-produc-
tive. You might as well do a roll call of things, and then you'd
realize that we're stuck with an outdated list, that no one's in
class anymore except for some self-portraits of death.

Are you still with me?

Yes, but it would be wise to slow down. Let's say that the
path opens suddenly, after the circular building, onto a canal
whose water is particularly high. There's no risk of drowning,
no danger of you lying down beside it and closing your eyes
and letting the noise of the current stir up the spray of your
memories. It was the autumn of electronic cigarettes with
exotic flavors. Every day had its mouth full of apples and we
flowed everywhere, or rather we knocked over our cocktails
everywhere. Later our friends and their colors began to dis-
tance themselves, one by one. In a black-and-white world of
goodbye, we watched the suspended particles of dust, trying
to find a name for them. But not yet. It was the autumn
when I loved you terribly, whoever you might be, because it
was now or never. In fact, I'm going to make you a vow: it is

already much too late to believe that a body is enough to con-
jugate each movement in the future tense. In any case, the
sweep of the landscape will no longer broaden, like on first
seeing it, remember how we had the impression that it would
always be enough to have just one ticket for two. This is what
he meant, the living ancient, when he said "in my days": the
time when you could set turnstiles of the possible spinning
endlessly. It was the autumn when everyone still added a
little to the directory of sexual names, but less and less.

Anyway, she stayed for longer than she had to, in the
square or the library or the museum, it doesn't matter. Maybe
it was because she refused to take up the verb to leave for
herself. The night gave the illusion of being at its height.
Someone leaned towards her and said, I had my arms full of
the Indian-summer wildflowers. What if the two of us made
up a speech in a new language we could still speak, and some
new animals? Her husband made no response but wasn't that
convenient, or even right, considering all those who hoped?

Later, one day—just another day, it doesn't matter which—
the paintings her husband bought in the galleries he vis-
ited dutifully all seemed to have left their frames. They
trailed over the ground like great puddles of viscous jelly.
Fortunately no one is ever completely without a sort of
Buddhist wisdom. A little quiet and some contemplation and
perhaps a scratch of the head and everything returns to order.
When she opened her eyes again, existence had regained its
general rhythm. It was the winter when the word took place
without the thing and even the snow was in the process of
disappearing. Having been the object of someone's love
once, even long ago, lets you resist everything, said the poet.
Time once again ran normally through her hands.

It was the winter when mothers taught their children to
draw on tablets. And she hadn't renounced figuring out the
number of signs necessary for continuity, either. In the past,
someone had told her something that she reconstituted, more
or less, as: "Each time my heart is broken I feel more adven-
turous, but soon I won't have enough [blank] to continue my

exploration." Was "resources" the word swallowed up by the blank? Conversation? Intimacy? In any case, now there was no trace at all of her husband, as if one night he took a wrong turn and ended up in another woman's vocabulary by accident.

Now everything was fluid. It was almost extraordinary. Of course she was still invited to a certain number of parties, and she showed up with carefully wrapped gifts which each contained the concise wisdom of a fortune cookie: here is a message for you. Everyone seemed to wish themselves that type of acolyte, vital and vibrating like something that talks and talks and doesn't leave room for anything else. It was the winter when we kept opening the front door because we heard the doorbell ring but that was revealed to an illusion and finally the doctors diagnosed us with clogged arteries. Doubtless we were lost. Someone kept repeating the Polish word for snow—*śnieg, śnieg*—as if language were able to make a blanket of white to cover the world.

—Do you think we'll find hands to apply to our bodies like hot, relaxing stones? The advertisements promised spas where everyone would be ignorant of the word *śmierć*, which means death. It was exactly at this moment that a woman cried, stop, because she was becoming ill with the dusk.

It was the winter when someone sang from morning to night to stop fear from coming back. We couldn't make heads or tails of anything anymore but we had to keep going because if she fell silent everything would seem horribly dramatic. Horribly or emphatically? It was the winter when we were alone with our favorite flower and the late echo of things. The rest was useless. Frankly it had no importance, and it made even less of a difference.

Grateful thanks to the editors of *World Literature Today* and *New Delta Review*, where excerpts from this translation first appeared.

Stéphane Bouquet is the author of eight collections of poetry, as well as essays on poetry. He has published books on filmmakers such as Sergei Eisenstein and Gus Van Sant, as well as screenplays for feature films, nonfiction films, and short films, and has translated poets including Paul Blackburn, James Schuyler, and Peter Gizzi into French. He's also interested in performance arts and has given workshops for choreographers at the Centre National de la danse in Paris and for actors and stage directors at La Manufacture in Lausanne, Switzerland. Bouquet is a recipient of a 2003 Prix de Rome and a 2007 Mission Stendhal Award, and has been featured in France and internationally at festivals, residencies, and events, including the 2017 Frankfurt Book Fair and the 2018 Toronto Festival of Authors. He holds an MA in economics from Université Panthéon-Sorbonne.

Lindsay Turner is the author of *Songs & Ballads* (2018) and *The Upstate* (forthcoming). Her translations from the French include books of poetry and philosophy by Stéphane Bouquet, Éric Baratay, Souleymane Bachir Diagne, Anne Dufourmantelle, Frédéric Neyrat, Ryoko Sekiguchi, and Richard Rechtman. She has twice received French Voices Grants for her translations. Originally from northeast Tennessee, she holds an AB from Harvard College, a Masters in cinema from the Université Paris III Sorbonne-Nouvelle, an MFA in poetry from New York University, and a PhD in English from the University of Virginia. She lives in Cleveland, where she is Assistant Professor in the English Department at Case Western University.

NIGHTBOAT BOOKS

Nightboat Books, a nonprofit organization, seeks to develop audiences for writers whose work resists convention and transcends boundaries. We publish books rich with poignancy, intelligence, and risk. Please visit nightboat.org to learn about our titles and how you can support our future publications.

The following individuals have supported the publication of this book. We thank them for their generosity and commitment to the mission of Nightboat Books:

Anonymous (4)
Kazim Ali
Abraham Avnisan
Jean C. Ballantyne
The Robert C. Brooks Revocable Trust
Amanda Greenberger
Rachel Lithgow
Anne Marie Macari
Elizabeth Madans
Elizabeth Motika
Thomas Shardlow
Benjamin Taylor
Jerrie Whitfield & Richard Motika

This book is made possible, in part, by grants from the New York City Department of Cultural Affairs in partnership with the City Council and the New York State Council on the Arts Literature Program.